THE MASTER'S MASTER

MY PERSONAL JOURNEY WITH GOD

BY
GRAND MASTER BILL JONES

The Master's Master

My Personal Journey with God

By
Grand Master Bill Jones

ABOOKS
Alive Book Publishing

Additional copies may be ordered from the publisher for
educational, business, promotional or premium use.
For information, contact ALIVE Book Publishing at:
alivebookpublishing.com, or call (925) 837-7303.

Book Design by Alex Johnson

ISBN-13: 978-1-63132-028-6
ISBN-10: 1-63132-028-9

Library of Congress Control Number: 201693476

Library of Congress Cataloging-in-Publication Data
is available upon request.

First Edition

The author believes that what comes from God is to be returned to
God, therefore procedes from this book shall be used to establish the
"Water for Life" ministry, to build wells throughout the world.

Published in the United States of America
by ALIVE Book Publishing and ALIVE Publishing Group,
imprints of Advanced Publishing LLC
3200 A Danville Blvd., Suite 204, Alamo, California 94507
alivebookpublishing.com

PRINTED IN THE UNITED STATES OF AMERICA

10 9 8 7 6 5 4 3 2 1

TABLE OF CONTENTS

DEDICATION

To my father, Jack, my mother, Maxine,
and my brother, Jackson.

You did more for me than you will ever know.

Acknowledgements

There are so many people to thank, I don't know where to start—but I will start here…

First of all, I thank Joyce Meyer, Pat Robertson, and K Love Radio Station for their powerful inspiration over the years. Their teaching, guidance and stories that helped me in my Christian walk in ways they will never know.

A special thanks to my family, friends, and all the people who prayed for me. Most special thanks to my good friend, Master Perrin, for without his help and dedication to assist me, I would have given up and closed my school.

I also thank Pastor Sami Shenouda for his valuable assistance with the scripture verses

I wouldn't be where I am at today without the love and support of my wife, Marie, my daughters, Jessica and Bianca, and my little dog, Corky.

Lastly, but most importantly, I thank my Lord and Master, Jesus Christ, for healing me, teaching me, guiding me, and blessing me in so many ways. His help along the way has been critical in making this book a reality. I want most of all to serve Him, and for this book to be a tool that He can use to bless others.

Remember that through God, all things are possible.

Because of Him, I am no longer a broken master.

INTRODUCTION

The Master's Master

This book is about the personal time that I have spent with God. He has taught me and has guided me through my difficult times. He has granted me many great miracles that he performed in my life and for others.

At one time, God told me to give up the martial arts and spread the word of the Lord. If you read this book, you will realize it would have been very difficult for me to do give up martial arts. I have been studying martial arts for more than fifty years. I understand that God wants me to finish this book, finish my music, go on special TV shows like *Benny Hinn, Joyce Meyers,* and *The 700 club,* and tell my stories about God in my book, sing my songs, sell them, collect the money and donations and then go on mission trips.

I'd like to help all the little children, build wells, feed the needy, help the homeless and do whatever else God wants me to do. Now just a little about me:

When I was little boy, before my stepfather passed away, he told me that if anything happened to him, to take care of my mother. Then he passed away. As a young boy I was inspired by men like James Bond, 007, and Bruce Lee .These men that were great heroes. They beat up the bad guys and protected the weak. They were black belts in four or five forms of martial arts. They were looked up to, admired and had beautiful women surrounding them at all times. I wanted to be a hero. I wanted to be a protector. I wanted to be that great man. I wanted to be a teacher and a leader. I wanted to encourage, and to inspire others. I wanted to help children and adults with special-needs. I wanted to be loved and be someone special—someone important.

I started martial arts in 1962 . I never expected to become who I am today. All I wanted at that time was to become a Black Belt. Since then, I have studied 14 forms of martial arts. I have received eight black belts, three master's degrees, ninth degree grand master, two PhD's in martial arts philosophy and science. I have won over 347 championships, 52 gold medals, 10 competitor-of-the-year awards, 17 world titles and I have been inducted into 13 different Halls of Fame across the world.

I have appeared in hundreds of magazines including a front cover story in *Black Belt Magazine* with the great Bruce Lee. I was in a movie called Weapon of Choice which I played myself, Master Jones. I received special awards from a four-star general, the FBI, and the President of United States. Say no more...Grand Master Bill Jones.

If you want to see more and read more about Master Jones, go to MasterBillJones.com or contact me at (925)-686-5425.

And the LORD, he it is that doth go before thee;
he will be with thee, he will not fail thee, neither forsake thee:
fear not, neither be dismayed.
Deuteronomy 31:8

CHAPTER 1

Hearing without Hearing; Seeing without Seeing; Touching without Touching"

People used to ask me, "How do you know when God is near?" I would tell them, "I know He is near by because I hear His voice and I know what it sounds like. I have felt His individual presence many times and know who He is." And people would ask, "How do you know when He is not speaking to you?" I tell them, "If you hear can hear God's voice as clearly as you can hear mine, you know He is not speaking because you don't hear anything."

Maybe this will help you understand:

When I was a young child, I was aware that I had special gifts. The first time I realized it, I was about six and a half years old. One day, just before leaving for school, my stepfather said, "Son, if anything ever happens to me, please be sure to take care of your mother." I then headed off to school.

After being at school for a while, I began to cry for no apparent reason. This was very unusual because I rarely ever cried at school. My teacher was so concerned, she called the school office to have my brothers and sister brought to our classroom, so that they might try to comfort me. When they arrived, they asked what was wrong and why was I crying, as I continued to sob, almost uncontrollably. Almost choking, I blurted out, "My daddy is dead! The man who raised me is dead!" They said, "Why would you say such a thing? What makes you think that?" I answered, "Because... he is standing right next to me. I know it!"

You see, I could feel his individual presence, just as I do when I feel God beside me. One of my gifts is being able to feel the energy of life that is separate from the body. That energy travels from one person to another, and moves independently from the body. Some people can sense or feel this, and it is even possible to photograph this individual energy presence, usually called and "aura."

If there are two people that were close to each other, like mom and dad or their children, their energy or their "aura" becomes one. If two people don't know each other and are standing beside one another, there is a separation between their energies.

We all have these special gifts, we just need to learn how to use them.

This is what I mean when I try to describe an individual presence or feeling. Auras can be seen and felt by people who have this special gift, and there is even a special camera that can actually take a picture of it, like pictures you sometimes see of Jesus.

Later in my life, when I was about fourteen years old, I actually died and came back to life. That definitely confirmed that God had given me some special gifts!

One of these gifts I call, "Seeing without seeing." What do I mean by this? This might help you to understand:

When someone tells a story, they physically and emotionally re-live that particular experience again in their mind. When they do this, they actual visualize the entire event. I can actually "see" that picture subconsciously, too! This is called "mental projection."

Other times, people sometimes think of saying something subconsciously but don't verbally say anything. I actually hear these thoughts and think they're talking to me, so I answer them. As you might imagine, this has caused a lot of complications in my relationships!

Many times, people think of things, not necessarily meaning it, but only thinking it, and I hear those thoughts. Again, I think they are speaking, so I answer them. This sometimes causes a lot of trouble.

I try now to be aware of this, and try my best not to do it anymore in my relationships, except with my children when I think I can help or guide them. Sometimes I ask my children, "Why do you think that way?"

Many times, when I am teaching, I can hear and know when people are *not* thinking. So, to help them, I explain that the mind must first *think*, before the body can respond or react. I'm not trying to make them feel bad; I'm only trying to help them. This gift I call, "hearing without hearing."

The next gift is "touching without touching." This is pretty cool, as it allows you to have the ability to touch something without physically touching it. This is actually quite easy. Just look at an object, then "touch" it in your mind. Is it hot, cold, soft, hard, bumpy or smooth? When you are done, walk over to it and physically touch it with your hand. See if it felt the same way as it did when you touched it with your mind. It is easy to develop this skill.

Many times people will come up to me and say, "I hurt my arm," or, "I hurt my leg," or, "I bumped my head." I will take my hand or finger and touch the spot and ask, "Right there?" They always ask me, "How did you know it was right there?" I tell them, "Because I can feel it." Where there is pain there is magnetic energy and heat. I can feel that energy.

All of these gifts were given to me by God. God said to me, "These gifts that I give you must not be used for your own satisfaction. You must use these gifts to help others."

These gifts help me when teaching people with disabilities like ADD, or hyperactive deficit disorder, dyslexia, bipolar disorder, autism, cerebral palsy, and more. God knew that without these gifts, many of the things that we try to accomplish would be difficult.

I thank God every day for blessing me with the ability to use these gifts in this way to help others.

God has never let me down. He has always been there for me when I have needed Him or His assistance. All praise and thanks be to God!

My sheep hear my voice,
and I know them, and they follow me.
John 10:27

Beloved, believe not every spirit,
but try the spirits whether they are of God:
because many false prophets are gone out into the world.
1 John 4:1

Now there are diversities of gifts,
but the same Spirit. And there are differences of
administrations, but the same Lord.
1 Corinthians 12:4-5

But the manifestation of the Spirit
is given to every man to profit withal.
1 Corinthians 12:7

And he gave some, apostles; and some, prophets; and some,
evangelists; and some, pastors and teachers;
For the perfecting of the saints, for the work of the ministry,
for the edifying of the body of Christ:
Ephesians 4:11-12

CHAPTER 2
The First Miracle

This is the first time that I remember ever asking God to be there for me and to help me. I was only six years old. I grew up with a lot of animals as a little boy but I never had a dog of my own. One day, several of my mom's friends went hunting in the mountains. They were attacked by a wolf and had to shoot it before it could harm them.

Soon after they killed the wolf, they could hear what sounded like little puppies barking and whining. They looked for them and soon found a small litter of young wolf pups. They figured the wolf they had killed must have been their mother, and knew the pups would not survive long left all alone, so they brought them back home.

They gave one of the wolf pups to me. We figured the little puppy must have been part wolf and part husky, because he didn't look like he was a fully wild wolf. He was black all over except for some white on his chest and on his little paws. I named him Sam.

At this time, my stepfather had since passed away, and all of my brothers and sisters had moved away. I was all alone. My mom had to work all day and often at night, so the only real companion I had was my dog, Sam. Because my stepfather had passed away, I felt pretty sad, and I could tell that my dog could sense it. For some reason, I was sure Sam was trying to comfort me.

Eventually, I realized that I had the ability to communicate with him through mental projection—that I could communicate with my dog without saying anything. This made me curious. So I asked myself, "Do dogs only talk to dogs, cats to cats, birds

21

to birds, or do all animals communicate with one another?"

I realized that by focusing my thoughts and listening carefully, I could hear them think and communicate with each other. Amazing! It was like there was a universal language through mental projection! It was then that I realized that I had the ability to communicate with animals through thought.

Later, when I would go to the mountains, I would allow my mind to think soft, loving thoughts, like the image of Snow White and the animals. The wild animals of the forest could sense these feelings, and they would come to me.

There were deer, squirrels, ducks, geese and all kinds of birds that would gather and eat from my hands, just like Snow White. This was unbelievable. What a beautiful gift from God!

One day, Sam and I were walking to the store. He used to always think that cars were other animals or something, and would try to chase them and bite their tires. As he was running across the street chasing a car, a big station wagon seemed to come out of nowhere and hit Sam, straight on at about 45 miles an hour, killing him.

Other cars stopped and people came out of their homes. I ran over and held him in my arms, but he was already dead. People tried to help me and wanted to take Sam from my arms, but I wouldn't let go. I just holding him and kept crying.

After what seemed like hours, they finally called the police and called animal control to have them take Sam away. But I still wouldn't let go. They showed me that Sam wasn't breathing and had been dead for a while and told me that I had a let him go, but again, I just wouldn't let go.

I looked up to God and said, "God please don't let my dog die. Let him wake up so I can take him home." Suddenly, as soon as I had spoken these words to God, Sam moved his eyes. I cried out, "Look everybody, he moved his eyes!" Everyone just stared and shook their heads, saying, "No son, that's impossible. He's dead. Let go so we can take him."

Then Sam moved his eyes again. I said, "No! Look, he moved his eyes again!" Again, the crowd said, "No son. Now, please let go." They then tried to pull Sam from my arms.

Suddenly, Sam stood up. He was alive! He had no cuts, bruises or broken bones. There was absolutely nothing wrong with him at all. I then stood up, Sam stood up and we started walking home. All of the people were amazed.

Many years later when my dog, Sam, did die, it touched my heart so much that I never had another pet for fifty years. Sam was a special companion and stayed with me for many years while I was young—all because of this miracle of God bring Sam back to life.

This was the first miracle that God did for me, and after it, I *knew* for certain that God was real, and that through God, all things were possible!

And all things, whatsoever ye shall ask in prayer,
believing, ye shall receive.
Matthew 21:22

Verily, verily, I say unto you, He that believeth on me, the works
that I do shall he do also; and greater works than these shall he do;
because I go unto my Father. And whatsoever ye shall ask in my
name, that will I do, that the Father may be glorified in the Son.
If ye shall ask any thing in my name, I will do it.
John 14:12-14

Jesus said unto him, If thou canst believe,
all things are possible to him that believeth.
Mark 9:23

CHAPTER 3
Letting Go

The first time in my life (and one of the hardest I can remember) was when I had to let go of something that I truly loved—my dog, Sam.

As I said before, the first miracle that God performed for me was bringing my dog, Sam, back to life. Now let me tell you the ending of the story. I was only about eight years old and I truly loved Sam more than anything in the world. We were best friends and best buddies. We did everything together. He was the joy of my life.

Sam used to stare out the window for hours and hours just waiting for me to come home from school. One time, I walked three miles to school. My mom had let Sam outside, and you know what? He tracked me those three miles, and ended up walking into my classroom and sitting beside me. It was amazing!

Sam would do anything to be with me. We could communicate with each other subconsciously (through mental projection), and we were always able to know and understand all the things that we each felt and thought. Every day when I would have to leave or go to school, Sam would just sit there and cry while I got ready to leave. He truly loved me. He would sit there for hours and hours, just staring out the window, waiting for me to come home.

Once, while I was growing up, we moved to Idaho. Besides Sam, we also had two little puppies. They brought joy to my heart. Sam was very protective of the two little puppies. One day, Sam and the two puppies were out in the front yard playing.

There were some stray dogs in the area that came into town

early in the morning and late at night, looking for food. Early one morning, as the wild dogs entered town, they spotted the two young puppies and started to slowly approach them. Sam noticed them coming and protected the puppies by killing the two stray dogs.

When the two dead dogs were examined, it was determined that they had rabies. Because Sam bit into the dogs, he would catch rabies too and we would have to put him to sleep before he could hurt anyone. My mom knew that this would really break my heart. She called a nearby animal hospital and asked them to send a truck, to come pick up Sam. She knew that if she put Sam in the car with us to go to the animal hospital, he would know what I was thinking as I started crying—that he would know that he was going to leave us.

Sam was a very smart dog. If we said, "You want to go bye-bye?" he would go grab his leash. If he was hungry, he would bring me his bowl. If he wanted water, he would bring me the other bowl. If we were going to go somewhere he would try to find the keys. Sam understood just about everything that I was thinking and feeling.

The animal control truck finally arrived. A man opened the back of the truck and told me to put the dog inside. I couldn't do it. Normally if I said, "Do you want to go bye-bye?" he would jump in the car. This time when I said, "Sam, you want to go bye-bye?" he would not jump in the truck. Instead, he looked at me, knowing what was going to happen and asked me, subconsciously, "Why? Why do you want me to go away?"

I said, "Sam there's nothing I can do for you. You have to go." He jumped in the truck and jumped back out. He wanted to give me love one more time! After I gave him lots and lots of love, he jumped in the truck. I shut the door and he stared at me. He used to cry every single time that we would be separated, but this time he didn't cry because he knew it would hurt me.

So, he held his head up high and stood strong. I knew this

was going to be very hard on me but there was nothing that I could do. Then the truck drove away.

Now I understand what it means to let go of something you love. This touched my heart so much that I have never had another animal in fifty years.

Next, there is a story about my wife. When I first met her, she already had a little dog called "Boots." My wife was thirty-eight at that time. She had never dated another man in her life, and Boots was the love of her life. Boots was an old dog—about fourteen—and that's very old for a dog. Boots had trouble with his heart. His heart grew too big and he was having trouble breathing. They would take him to the veterinarian, time after time.

Everyone in the family would gather together and pray for him. He would get better, and the doctor would let him go home. This happened over and over again. In my eyes, I felt that the dog was suffering and so did my brother-in-law. To me, it was more important to think about what the dog was going through than about how they felt about letting him go with God.

One day, when my wife took Boots to the doctor, the doctor was amazed. He said that the dog's heart had shrunk and there was nothing wrong with him anymore. So we all decided to go camping and take him with us. He played like he was a little puppy again, running and jumping and having no trouble breathing. This was amazing. God was letting him enjoy his life one more time to the fullest, before it would be time for him to leave.

Time went on and he started having trouble breathing again. This was very difficult for me because I cared a lot for the little dog too. Boots then started spitting up blood, so we realized that there was something really wrong with him. We took him to the vet again and everybody prayed. Again, the doctor let the dog go back home.

On the way home, Boots started spitting up blood again, so we turned around and headed back to the doctor. I looked up to God and said, "God if you're not going to heal this little dog, please do not let him suffer anymore. Please let everybody make the right decision for what is best for boots." Everybody knew that this would be one of the most difficult times for me as well as everybody else.

They decided to have Boots put to sleep. They had to let go and set him free, so they all gathered around him and gave him love as he fell asleep. This affected everybody, but especially my wife because Boots was the love of her life. I remembered how it affected me when I lost my dog, Sam, so we comforted each other as we struggled through this difficult time. I was praying for them all during this time.

My wife, too, now understands what it means to let go or set free of something you love and cherish. I had to do the same thing for my brother, my mom, and my dad. It was painful to see all three of them suffer so much. In every case, in the end, I would pray to God and say, "God, if you're not going to heal them completely, please set them free, like the wind."

I had to learn to let go of what I felt, because of course, I didn't want to lose my mom, dad, or brother. My mom really wanted to be set free. She didn't want to suffer anymore. She even asked me and my wife how she could have a close relationship with God. It was a beautiful thing to learn that my mom, dad and brother all found salvation in their lives, just days before they died!

Some doctors have told me that there is no cure, treatment, therapy or recovery, for my condition, and that different parts of my body will shut down and that I will go into a coma and die. At this time, half of my right leg is numb and my left leg is not working very well. My left foot and my left arm don't work at all. I have trouble focusing my thoughts when I have to concentrate.

I really do not want to fall apart like this. I told my wife and children that if these things happen to me—that if I fall into a coma, —please don't allow me to just sit there, suffering. I know they'll miss me and I will miss them too. They need to think about how I'm feeling and what I've gone through. They will have to let me go and be with God. No more suffering—free, like the wind! All I ask is that they place their hands on me, so I know they are there—for my wife to rub my head, so I know she's beside me.

And then, unplug me, setting me free. Now you will truly understand what it means to let go of something you love and cherish.

That if thou shalt confess with thy mouth the Lord Jesus, and shalt
believe in thine heart that God hath raised him
from the dead, thou shalt be saved.
Romans 10:9

For whosoever shall call upon the name
of the Lord shall be saved.
Romans 10:13

CHAPTER 4

The Seven Days: A Day with the Tree
and a Day with the Lord

A young boy and his father were cutting down a tree. A strong wind was blowing and the tree fell in the wrong direction, landing upon the child and crushing him. Blood came out of his ears and nose, and even from his eyes. When the ambulance arrived, they said that he was clinically dead. His name was Eric.

Eric started practicing martial arts with me when he was only four years old. At the time of the accident he was about nine years old. He was one of our junior black belts—a very skilled, young man, who had won hundreds of championships as well as the competitor of the year award. After the accident his parents asked me to come to the hospital because they knew Eric was used to hearing my voice. They thought there could be a possibility that he could hear me and could respond to me. He was in a coma.

After I got there to comfort his parents and the other children, I put my hands on him and realized there was no reaction from him in anyway. The hospital had him on life support, but essentially, he was brain dead. I went to see him every day, so that I could meditate and pray over him. I would place my hands on him and give him the spirit of life; the energy that kept me alive. I would take all of the negative energy, the Spirit of Death, from Eric, with me so that I could release it.

I would then go to a special place, deep in the mountains, to release the negative energy. I would have to climb over rocks and dangerous areas to get to the special tree—a tree that I call The Tree of Life.

You see, everything in this world is made up of magnetic,

electrical energy. This is true for trees, as well. The bigger the tree, the more the energy it has. I would place my hands on the tree and punch and kick the tree, over and over again, to release all of the negative energy. Then, when I was done, I would place my hands back on the tree, pray and meditate and allow the tree to fill me with positive energy.

Because the tree was so much bigger than me, it could easily absorb all the negative energy, then fill me with positive energy. Every time I would sit down to meditate and pray, I would often cry, too. When I did, a little bird would always appear on the same branch and sing a very special song. I knew that the angels were trying to let me know that everything was going to be okay.

I went to the tree for over year, and eventually began to mentally fall apart. I started having anxiety and panic attacks, and even had a hard time teaching the children during this time. I also became emotionally disturbed, crying a lot as I thought about Eric. For a while, I even became homeless, and slept on the floor in the back room of my karate school. I believed I was starting to die.

During this time, another one of the junior black belts from my Martial Arts Academy named Jackson, also a great champion, suffered a brain aneurysm and lapsed into a coma. Like Eric, he also was only nine years old. He was sent to a different hospital. Again, his parents asked me if I could go to the hospital as well, because they knew Jackson was also used to my voice and there was a possibility that he could hear me or respond to me.

He did respond, so we all knew he was still alive, although he was still in a coma. Now I was going to two different hospitals; one in San Francisco for Eric and one in Oakland for Jackson. This was very hard on me. I had to go visit both children at the hospitals, day after day, pray and meditate over them, and then go to the Tree of Life.

At this time, my mother had two different bypasses and

started to die. She was in Chico—even farther away—so now it was even more difficult for me to try to go to all three different hospitals, as often as possible, and share with them the spirit of life that I would get from the tree.

Once again, I began to fall apart and felt as though I wanted to die. I was having anxiety and panic attacks 20 to 30 times a day. I would call my daughter and say, "Jessica, please tell me that I'm okay; please just tell me that I'm okay." Just hearing her voice always helped me through, as she let me know that she was always there for me.

I went to the priest and asked him to pray over me. The told me that I needed to go to the hospital but I told him I didn't want to go. So he put his hands over me and prayed. "God please help this Man."

All along, I offered God my personal self as a sacrifice and to take me so that the two children could live. I had prayed every day for God's strength and help. At that time I shaved my head and didn't eat food for eight days—not a single bite. I went to the mountains to pray.

I could hear little children laughing and playing in the park. It made me think about all the little kids at my Tae Kwon Do school. It hurt me a lot because I was losing my ability to teach them and it made me cry. This hurt me the most of all because I love my karate kids.

I looked up to God and said, "God when I wake up in the middle of the night and have a panic attack, I have nobody." God said, "Yes you do. You have your daughter." This made me cry. So I then decided to walk deep, deep into the mountains, where there are no bicycle trails or walking trails; through the rocks, sticks and bushes, as far as I could go, so that nobody could hear me cry. It was deep in the winter time, so no leaves were on the trees. It was windy, freezing cold and raining hard. After about an hour of walking deep in the mountains, I came to a big tree. It had broken branches beside it. I grabbed a huge broken branch and swept the ground to make it clean. I moved all the rocks, sticks, and twigs so there would be nothing in my way.

I then sat down beside the tree in the mud, in the pouring rain, and prayed, cried, and meditated for about an hour. I was wet, muddy, and cold. I looked up to God and said, "God, when I wake up in the middle of the night and go through all these attacks and anxiety, and my daughter is not there, I have no one." God then said, "Yes you do. I'm right here beside you." This is the first time that I really actually heard God's voice out loud. I knew He was right beside me but as I looked up to the side of me, I saw no one. I bowed my head and started to cry, but as I did, I saw, underneath my arm, a teddy bear—about a foot tall, all white and brand-new. It wasn't wet or muddy—just a beautiful, little white teddy bear with a red bow, and arms and legs that moved. I knew it was God. There was no way that in the winter, deep in the mountains and in the rain, that someone had come and left that bear there, under that tree. It was not there when I cleaned the area.

I know that we are not to worship objects, but I knew then that God was trying to tell me that when I thought that I was all alone, I wasn't, and that all I would have to do to realize this was look at that bear. I know that God was always beside me.

I took the bear back home and within seven days, both Eric and Jackson came out of their comas and were once again, fully alive. Eric was clinically dead for a very long time. Jackson was in a coma for months.

The LORD is nigh unto all them that call upon him,
to all that call upon him in truth.
Psalm 145:18

Who his own self bare our sins in his own body on the tree,
that we, being dead to sins, should live unto righteousness:
by whose stripes ye were healed.
1Peter 2:24

CHAPTER 5

The Red Rose

When I was about 14 years old, I was a very strong and healthy young man. I was working in a restaurant, going to school, and doing martial arts. I was also a flight Sergeant in the ROTC (Reserve Officer Training Core) at Travis Air Force Base. What a great honor it was for a young man as I was also competing in the Marine Corps youth physical fitness team at the Alameda Naval Station. I was a very busy young man.

While doing martial arts, I learned about what is called "Chi" or internal strength. I also learned about the "meditation of strength," which is controlling the mind over the body's physical ability. The mind has the ability to control 80% of both strength and weakness. Controlling the mind allows one to control more energy than the body can normally accept.

One day I was lifting weights using this method. I could lift 780 pounds with my legs and 450 pounds with one leg. I could also lift 380 pounds in the bench press, 210 pounds standing press, and 180 pounds on the bicep curls. I was very, very strong.

I was coming back from lunch when, all of a sudden, I didn't feel well. I fell to the ground. I knew something was wrong, as I wasn't strong enough to stand up, lift my arms, or even get up and try to get some help.

Someone saw me and picked me up. They took me to the school, to the nurse's office. After I got to the office, the nurse examined me and didn't know what was wrong. At the time, I had a terrible headache and was very weak. The nurse decided to call my parents to tell them that she was going to take me home.

When she dropped me off, I was still very weak. I decided to lie down in my backyard because I thought maybe I might vomit. When my mom and dad came home, they couldn't find me at first because I was in the backyard. When they finally found me, they could tell something was wrong. They picked me up and took me to the hospital in Fairfield.

The hospital in Fairfield couldn't figure out what was wrong with me, so they placed me in an ambulance and rushed me to Napa Queen Valley Hospital. They didn't know what was wrong with me, but thought there was a possibility that I wouldn't make it and die. When they finally got me to get hospital, they did x-rays, an EKG, placed 23 needles in my head, and ran electricity through me. They did so many tests, that I can't explain what they were all called.

Since they still couldn't figure out what was wrong and why I might actually be dying, they asked my mom if she would allow them to do anything and everything and that they would actually pay for it. They had never seen anything like this before. They put me in the ICU for three days. My heart slowed down to about six times a minute. After some time, they still couldn't figure out what was wrong. They took my mom aside and told her they didn't know what to do since my heart was slowing down so much. They said they thought I might only last another day.

At that moment, a nun came in the room and asked if there was anything that she could do for me. I told her I wanted a priest, so she called for one.

When he arrived, the priest prayed over me. He prayed the words of salvation, preparing me just in case I didn't make it. Then the nun came back and said, "You're too young to be here," and gave me a red rose, which stands for eternal life. I was having a hard time staying awake. I started closing my eyes but I tried to keep them open so I could look at everything around me one more time. I knew that if I closed my eyes, there was a possibility that I was going to die. I began to slip away.

I started dreaming of all the things that I wanted to do as I got older, like becoming a black belt in karate, getting married, and having children. I then realized that I wasn't really dreaming. God was showing me my future, if only I continued living. He offered me a choice; to go with him or to go back to my life on earth. I said, "God I don't want to die. I want to go back."

I saw beautiful lights and heard voices leading me back home. I remembered that before I closed my eyes, I was weak—so weak that I couldn't even lift my arms to wipe the tears from my eyes. But I did open my eyes, and was greeted with the greatest surprise to realize that it was no longer a dream. God sent me back and allowed me to live and to finish my journey in life. All during this time, all the monitors that were connected to my body had already started activating again and alarms were ringing out as I started slipping away.

When the doctors rushed into the room, they couldn't find me at first and asked the old man in the other bed beside me where I was. He said, "I think he's on the other side of the bed doing push-ups!" The doctors were amazed as they picked me up and checked me top try and figure out what had just happened. They kept me in the hospital for two more days and ran many tests one me, but never found anything wrong with me. I was then released and was able to go home. I was 14 years old. This was the second miracle that God did for me.

To better understand this miracle, be sure to read my story, "The Unknown: Understanding the Presence of God."

And said, If thou wilt diligently hearken to the voice
of the LORD thy God, and wilt do that which is
right in his sight, and wilt give ear to his commandments,
and keep all his statutes, I will put none of these diseases
upon thee, which I have brought upon the Egyptians:
for I am the LORD that healeth thee.
Exodus 15:26

CHAPTER 6
Miracles of God

When I was a young child my father and brothers drove motorcycles, and when I became older, I got one too. One time, I was driving my motorcycle to Lake Berryessa. As I drove along, I came to a stretch of road that was being worked on; they were putting new tar and gravel down.

As I came around a corner, going too fast, I crashed my motorcycle. I slid on the pavement and my motorcycle landed on top of me. It took off half of my right arm and almost all of my left arm, shoulder, hip, and part of my leg. No one was around, so I had to get back on my motorcycle and drive 30 miles to the hospital. I was badly hurt and it was very difficult.

When I arrived at the hospital, they rushed me into the emergency room. The doctors couldn't give me any painkillers because I had hurt too many parts of my body and they needed to act quickly to stop all the bleeding. They had to clean all my open wounds with iodine and cut out all the gravel and remove the tar that was stuck to me. Then they covered half of my body with bandages and sent me home.

I couldn't use my arms for a year and eight months as they were partially paralyzed. I couldn't feed myself or bathe myself. I thought I would never be able to do martial arts again. Then, through prayer, God healed me.

In another incident, a newspaper wrote a story about me and said that I broke more bones than Evel Knievel. I went to a chiropractor who said that I had damaged twelve vertebrate in my back and seven in my neck and I had no reflexes on the right side of my body. I used to go to the chiropractor three times a week. Through the martial arts, I strengthened myself and now I only go to the chiropractor twice a year.

When I was about 15 years old I wore five pound leg weights on each leg. I did this for about two years. One day while practicing, my brother said, "Do you think you could kick that target way up there and keep one leg on the ground?" The target was about six feet in the air. I said, "Sure." I took off my leg weights and kicked straight at the target. The extreme movement of this kick pulled my leg out of its socket and my right side became paralyzed. I thought I would never be able to do martial arts again, ride a bike, run after my children, play Frisbee, or swim. It took me over three yeas to learn to walk again, and a full eight years to run.

Again by praying for many years, God decided to heal me.

I also loved to go canoeing. One year I canoed a hundred and thirty-eight miles in five days. On the third day, I crashed against the rocks and my canoe flipped over. I lost all my food, water, and all my clothes. The pressure of the water was so strong that it stripped all the clothes off me. The water created pressure in my ears and I couldn't hear at all.

After this accident, I went to the doctor because I started having panic attacks, and no matter what the doctors did, I still couldn't hear for three months. Again, I prayed to God and he healed me.

Another time I started losing my vision. I couldn't even see the children in my class right beside me, and I couldn't read the signs along the highway. I was going blind! I went to doctors and specialists. They made me a pair of progressive glasses that helped a little, but I was still almost blind. I went home and kneeled down beside my bed and looked up to God. I said, "God I don't want to wear these glasses." I looked above my bed and there was a light shaped like a cross on the ceiling. It was about five feet wide and eight feet long—it was a perfect cross.

I could see that cross for about three months. It would appear every day on my ceiling. I would try to move everything in my bedroom to see what it might be, but I could never figure out where the light was coming from. As I continued praying to God, he ended up healing me, and I never did have to wear the glasses. My daughter used to say, "Daddy you paid four hundred dollars for those glasses and you never wear them. Why?" I would tell her, "Because God healed me, I don't need them." She was amazed. She was only three years old but already she was beginning to understand about God's amazing power to heal.

I've been healthy most all my life aside from being injured at different times. My heart beats at about 56 times per minute and my blood pressure is 102/70. No clogging in my arteries. I'm a very healthy man.

On November 22, 2009, I began studying jujitsu, a form of martial arts. I was 53 years old at that time. As we were rolling (like sparring in martial arts), I hurt my arm in what is called an "arm bar." I put a brace on my arm and continued training like that for one year. I had very little normal use of my arm and was not getting better. I went to my doctor who suggested that I see a neurologist. He examined me and said someone must have pulled on my arm and overstretched the nerve. It would take about three years to heal. My arm was shaking a lot. The doctor asked me if anybody in my family had any neuromuscular conditions. I told him that my mom had Parkinson's. Then the Neurologist said, "You have Parkinson's."

I tried everything to get better. I had several MRIs. I tried reflexology and acupuncture. The doctors did a nerve conductive study and more tests, including several ultrasounds. I went to three different chiropractors, two ART specialists who also tried red laser light therapy and even electric shock treatment. I went to another neurologist at Stanford University—the list goes on and on.

After all of those tests and treatments, the doctors said it was nerve damage, brain damaged tissue, Parkinson's, and the last MRI indicated that I may have *encephalomalacia,* which means damage to the brain. There is no treatment, no therapy, no cure, and no recovery. They told me that, eventually, different parts of my body and organs would shut down, that I would go blind, go into a coma, and then, in as little as seven days, I would die.

I also just learned that I have cancer. I don't know what's next! After all of this, I can only look back at all of the other times God healed me when the "experts" said there was no hope—time when I was "supposed" to die, but did not. Once again, I will leave it to God—and when God heals me of all these things it will be a great ending of this book!

Remember that it is important to pray every day. Never give up. Keep your faith. Always believe and trust in God. Through God, all things are possible.

Be careful for nothing; but in everything
by prayer and supplication with thanksgiving
let your requests be made known unto God.
Philippians 4:6

For verily I say unto you, That whosoever shall say unto this
mountain, Be thou removed, and be thou cast into the sea; and shall
not doubt in his heart, but shall believe that those things which he
saith shall come to pass; he shall have whatsoever he saith.
Mark 11:23

CHAPTER 7
Healing

In trying to recover, I not only visited 40 different doctors and specialists and three university medical centers, but also ten different ministries, six catholic churches and ten Priests, and attended fifteen different healing services. I was anointed more than ten times for healing, but still didn't see any improvement at that time.

Most doctors said to me, "I can't believe after all this time you haven't given up." I said, "I can't. It has all ready taken me four years to recover only a third of my physical ability, so I can't quit now." Little by little these changes only occurred through prayer and my faith in God—not through doctors or medicine. Over the past six years, I have recovered about 50% of my ability. Through God all things are possible.

One of the most exciting healing services I went to was in 2013. This Mario Murillo healing ministry was blessed so much by God's presence that they decided to write a newsletter about it which stated, "Concord California: It was not that God showed up, it was the way that he showed up."

During the service, one of the pastors noticed me in the crowd with my hands in the air, praying to God. He noticed that my arm was shaking. Doctors had said that I have nerve and brain damage; possibly even Parkinson's. The minister pointed to me and said, "Go to that man right there with this hand shaking. That man has the spirit of infirmity. I want all of you and the pastors to go lay your hands on that man right now." I couldn't say anything. I could only put my hands over my eyes and cry. All the people started talking in tongues. It sounded like 50 people. It was one of the most unusual things I had ever heard.

At the end of the service the minister said, "If there's anybody in this room that God has healed, I want you to stand up." This was the first time I ever did. After a couple weeks, my wife received a letter from the Ministry. It mentioned about the healing of the people that were there. There was a picture in the letter. A caption on the photo said, "Pastor Jim Carpenter feels a surge of miracle power as he prayed for this man." I looked at the picture and started crying because I realized it was me with my hands up, praising God, crying.

That weekend I went camping and as I was praying to God, he said, "You've already been healed. Now, you just need to recover." Then he said, "You're going to swim across Lake Berryessa on your birthday with both your arms and legs." At that time I really couldn't do that as my left arm and leg didn't work very well. It was very difficult as I tried to swim across the lake. It's about a half-mile across and, of course, a half-mile back. I normally wear a life jacket, just to make sure I'm safe, because one time I almost drowned.

I was excited. My friend, Mike, and I took his boat out to the middle of the lake, which was pretty far. He dropped anchor and I decided that I was going to see if I could swim with both my arms and legs. I took off my lifejacket, jumped in the water, and began to swim. I only made it about 20 feet when I realize I was about to drown. I must have gone under the water ten or more times and started screaming for help.

But my friend Mike had lost his hearing-aid and couldn't hear me as the boat started drifting away. The anchor wasn't holding and the boat was drifting away faster than I could swim towards the boat. I screamed and yelled for help but nobody could hear me. Finally, a woman on the boat realized that I was calling for help and threw me a life jacket.

It took me quite a while to get to the boat, but thanks to God, I didn't drown. I prayed to God and said, "God, I thought I was supposed to swim across the lake with both my arms and both my legs on my birthday." God answered, "You made two mistakes. The first mistake is that it was to be next year on your birthday, not this year, and the second mistake was, I told you would swim across the lake, but I didn't say 'without your life jacket.'" I always knew God had a great sense of humor!

On December 28, 2013, my wife invited me to another healing service. I had been to this healing service two times before and during one of those times, the priest said that he felt a surge of miracle power as he prayed over me. But this was to be the third time—and as they say, "The third time's a charm."

And it was really exciting because this time, as always, the minister spotted me in the crowd. He would always personally pray over me for healing and asked the other pastors and the congregation to gather around me and put their hands on me for healing. I told the minister, "Thank you for always making me feel like I'm not forgotten—that God knows I'm here and wants to heal me." Well this time was no different. At the end when the minister started healing people he looked over and there I was, standing there crying, with my hands in the air, worshiping God. "You see that man right there," he said, "I want all of you to go to him. I want you to put your hands on him so that God will know where to heal him."

My wife put her hands on my shoulder. I put one hand on my own shoulder and one hand on the side of my head. My arm was shaking tremendously. Everybody started praying and talking in tongues. There were many hands on me and all of a sudden, someone put his hands on my shoulder and it felt very, very hot. The minister said, "God please heal this man of his nerve damage and his damaged muscles." Then another man placed his hand on my shoulder and it was very hot, too. Then he said, "And heal this man's brain cells." Another man placed his hand on my head and his hand was also hot. I've never felt anything like that in my life.

The man that placed his hand on my head said to my wife,

"His head is so hot." So I didn't know if it was his hand that was hot or my head! People say that when God heals you, it almost feels like fire. It was very hot—hotter than a cup of coffee. I felt like I was going to pass out, but I knew that I mustn't give up. I knew God had special plans for me and that I had to be patient. It's God's timing not mine.

Now, I am looking forward to what's going to happen next. We must all have faith; we must not give up. We must continue to believe that through God, all things are possible.

One of the greatest people that I enjoy listening to and am inspired by is Joyce Meyer. One day, she said something that was a perfect answer to many of the questions that I had with all the different things that I've been going through. I would like to share that with you.

This is by Joyce Meyers (not by me):

I don't think that God always does everything in our life immediately. He wants us sometimes to go through enough to really appreciate Him when we get our breakthrough. I think God gives us enough time to completely wear ourselves out so when that breakthrough comes, we know that it was God and not us and we will never be tempted to take the credit. There will be things to go through but God will come through at the right time.

She says to read 1 Peter 5:10;

And after you have suffered a little while, God of all grace (who imparts all blessings and favors) who has called you to his (own) eternal glory in Christ Jesus, will himself, complete and make you what you ought to be; establish and ground you securely, and strengthen and settle you.

But the God of all grace, who hath called us
unto his eternal glory by Christ Jesus,
after that ye have suffered a while, make you perfect,
establish, strengthen, settle you.
1 Peter 5:10

CHAPTER 8
The Face of God

God is always looking over us, in the morning and at the night. All we have to do is look up at heaven and pray and he will hear our prayers.

One night I started praying to God. I was looking down at the lake and God said, "You missed. Turn your face and look at me." I didn't know what he meant. I turned around and looked behind me but didn't see anything. It was a full moon that night. When I looked at it, I thought about it for a moment. I realized it was the Face of God himself. I thought, "How could that be the face of God?"

When we say, "The Father, the Son, and Holy Ghost," we're talking about God. When you look at the moon, it is actually the reflection of the sun, which I believe represents God.

It says in the Bible that you can't look at God, because if you did, you would become blind—just like if you stare at the sun. The Bible also says that God is so bright that you shouldn't lift your head up and look at him—just like the sun.

So this is my understanding of what it means when we say, "The Father, the Son and the Holy Ghost." I understand that the Sun represents something different in the Bible, so please don't confuse yourself as I share my story.

In the daytime when we look for God, we know he's there because we can see the sun. But, at nighttime, we see the moon— the face of God. What I'm trying to say is: If the moon is a reflection of the sun, maybe the sun has a face on it too. We can only see it when we look at the moon—the reflection of God's face. That's why they say God is always smiling down on us.

As you read this book, you'll see that there are many miracles performed by God — some big and some small. Let me list a few:

The first one was when my dog had been hit by a car that had been going 45 miles per hour. He was dead for over two hours, when God brought him back to life.

The second one was when I was 14 years old, when I also died but God brought me back to life.

The next one was when Eric, who the newspapers stated that he was clinically dead for a year and eight months, was also brought back to life by a miracle of God.

Next, Jackson had a brain aneurysm and for eight months was in a coma. God brought him back, too.

When my father was in a coma for five days, the doctors told me nine times he was going to die, yet God kept him alive and brought him out of his coma.

When my brother, Jack, was found dead, he remained that way for an entire day. We prayed over him and cried, and God brought him back to life.

The next story is about my step-father's father, Bob…

My mother had heard about many of the miracles that had happened in my life through God, so she called me once and said, "Son, my father-in-law has not spoken in five years. We're afraid that he's going to die. Is there any way that you could pray for him so he can talk to us, so we can figure out what we can do and what he needs before he dies?" I didn't hear this from my mother personally, as she left this as a message on my phone. I started to pray. I saw a vision and heard God saying that Bob's dad would be able to talk but then he would die within a few days. About an hour later my mother called me back. She said, "Son, I can't believe it — he's talking." I told her what God told me, about Bob's dad dying. A few days later he died.

Next story is about a student named Nelson who attended my martial arts school. He had trouble with his kidneys and had to go to dialysis. He had to carry a pouch with him at all times.

He needed a kidney transplant. One day he told me, "Master Jones, my sister is going to give me one of her kidneys so I can live better." He went to the hospital and they began preparing him for the surgery. After a while, he started having complications.

The doctors had told him that there was a possibility that he might die during the surgery, so he decided to call me so I could be there with him at the hospital. While I was there, I prayed over him. They never did do the surgery as he recovered fully. He no longer needed to carry the pouch, as God healed him.

The next story is about a man named Steve. Steve came to me saying that God brought him there to be healed. I asked him what was wrong and he said that he'd been in a motorcycle accident and that he had twelve bolts, each four inches long, in his back to support his spine. I told him he wasn't ready to be with me yet. About four months later, he came back and said he had to be there at my karate school. He said that God told him to come so he could be healed. The doctors told him that because of his severe accident they could never remove the bolts from his back and that he would be like that for life.

The accident had crushed most of his vertebrae. After a few months of training and therapy through martial arts, he went back to the doctors and they removed all of the bolts—every single one of them. He put all the bolts in a jar and he's living a normal life, thanks to God. There was even a special story about him in the *Contra Costa Times* newspaper showing him holding the jar full of bolts!

*Is any sick among you? let him call for the elders of the church;
and let them pray over him, anointing him with oil
in the name of the Lord. And the prayer of faith
shall save the sick, and the Lord shall raise him up;
and if he have committed sins, they shall be forgiven him.*
James 5:14-15

CHAPTER 9
Tim Mahoney and God's Provision

One day, a homeless man came into my martial arts school. He said that God led him there and that martial arts could help change his life. He didn't have any money and he was in need of a shower. I decided to help him by giving him some items that he could use to get cleaned up with, along with a martial arts uniform so he could begin his training.

His uniform only lasted about two weeks as it seemed to simply deteriorate by having him wear it. I don't know for sure, but I think he was living in it, as martial arts became his way of life. I gave him another one.

He used to collect cans and would offer me money, but he needed the money a lot more than I did, so I wouldn't accept it. After several months, he got a job and I let him pay just a little bit so he could feel better about the situation. One day, he started crying. I asked him why he was crying. He answered, "My mom and dad haven't seen me in 17 years because of my alcohol and my drug abuse. They are coming today to watch me do martial arts."

His parents watched him do martial arts and saw the different man that he had become. He had discipline, respect, a purpose and a positive direction in life; no drugs or alcohol. They were so impressed, that later, when his mother died, she put it in her will that his martial arts were paid for, for life.

Some time later, he met a beautiful woman and got married. He bought a brand new truck. I never had a brand new truck and was jealous. Then, he bought a home, opened his own business and now lives happily ever after. This is true story about a homeless man named Tim Mahoney.

The next two stories were told to me by a priest and they also are true stories.

There was a priest and he bought some land that was on a big hill. We went to a contractor and asked him how much money it would take to level off the land to build a church. The company said one million dollars. The priest said, "I don't have that kind of money. I don't know what I'm going to do." He prayed to God.

Remember it is written that if it's God's will it's God's bill. That means that when God has plans for you to do something, he will take care of all your needs to accomplish whatever it is He has planned for you—financially, mentally, and physically.

Sometime later, a man walked up to the priest and said, "Excuse me sir, who owns this land?" The priest responded, "I do." The man then said, "Well, I'm building a bridge down the road and I need a lot of dirt and am willing to pay for it." The priest said, "I'll make you a deal. You level off the land for me to build my church and you can have all the free dirt you want." Remember, if it's God's will it's Gods bill.

The next story is about a young boy. He was at school and the teacher said, "Children, we are going to collect money for the homeless. Is there anybody who would like to help?" Johnny lifted his hand up and said, "I'll help get money for the homeless." His teacher was pleased and told him, "Good job, Johnny."

When class was over, she took Johnny aside and said, "Remember Johnny, whatever you do, don't go home and ask your parents for that money." Johnny didn't know what to do next because that's what he was planning to do. He went home and prayed, "God, please help me get some money so I could help the homeless people.

The weekend passed and his cousins came to visit him. Everyone got together and they went into town to go shopping.

When they were walking along, Johnny's aunt said, "I think I have something stuck on the bottom of my shoe." Johnny said, "I'll get it for you." He reached down and pulled it off. It was a dollar bill. Then Johnny remembered that he had prayed to God for some money so he could give it to the homeless people. He received it. The lesson learned is, if you trust in God all things are possible.

Except the LORD build the house,
they labour in vain that build it:
except the LORD keep the city,
the watchman waketh but in vain.
Psalm 127:1

CHAPTER 10
Thanksgiving

One day, several weeks before Thanksgiving, someone gave me a twenty pound turkey. I didn't know what to do with it. I woke up at three o'clock in the morning and decided to cook the turkey. The turkey was done by seven o'clock in the morning.

I was a single bachelor at the time, with no one to share it with. About two weeks before Thanksgiving, I was looking for my brother so I could bring him home to enjoy Thanksgiving with our family, but I couldn't find him. When Thanksgiving arrived, I got up early that morning and decided to look for him again, but I still couldn't find him.

I even went to the police station to see if I could find him there. The police told me that there were some of the homeless people back near the Martinez Marina, so I went there. I found a few homeless people as I got there and asked them if they had seen my brother. They knew who he was, but nobody had seen him.

I asked them if I could share my Thanksgiving dinner with them. They were happy to accept and said, "Absolutely. Thank you." So I went home and got the turkey and stuffing, some pumpkin pie and whipped cream, mashed potatoes and gravy, and everything else needed so we could enjoy our Thanksgiving together. I went back to the marina, but when I got there, I realized that about thirty 30 people had gathered there.

We all came together and prayed to God for this meal. After saying grace, I began cutting up the turkey and serving all of them, including several dogs. What a beautiful Thanksgiving. We never ran out of food and they took all leftovers home. I was reminded of the story about Jesus feeding the multitudes with just a few loaves of bread and a few fish. That is one of the most amazing stories in the Bible.

When I got home, I said to myself, "I never even made a plate for myself." Then I realized that the turkey wasn't meant for me—it was intended for me to share with all the homeless people so they could have a Great Thanksgiving too.

Later, I told my students about my story and my experience with the homeless. They were so excited, that they all decided to go with me the following year. The parents of my students, my wife, and all the children came to assist me. Everyone brought different kinds of food to enjoy. We had many different varieties of food to enjoy; three turkeys, four baked hams, 22 pies, and about fifty pounds of mashed potatoes, and so many desserts, I could hardly believe it.

I recall that we only had one, very small pitcher of gravy and was concerned that the gravy would run out because we had about fifty people to feed. I was going to ask that everyone limit themselves to a very small portion, but never got to mention it. But, amazingly, the gravy never did run out. Amazing! I was again reminded of the story of the loaves and fishes.

Before we started serving, we all gathered around and prayed together. It was funny. As we were praying, I looked around to see all the people. I glanced over and noticed my father had joined us. At first, I thought he was one of the homeless people. I said, "Dad, what are you doing here?" He replied, "I heard that the food was good."

What a blessing to have my father there with me. I was so busy taking care of the homeless people, and looking for my brother, that I forgot about my father. With all the people that my father knew, I'd thought he'd have many places to go for Thanksgiving. However, he chose to be with all of us, instead.

It was a blessing having everyone come to assist me, and help me with the homeless, and to have my father with us.—but most of all, it was a blessings to have God with us. What a beautiful Thanksgiving it was. Amen.

For I was an hungered, and ye gave me meat:
I was thirsty, and ye gave me drink:
I was a stranger, and ye took me in:
Naked, and ye clothed me:
I was sick, and ye visited me:
I was in prison, and ye came unto me.
Mt 25:35-39

CHAPTER 11
What Train are you Going Home on Today?

One day, I asked God what His voice sounds like. When God to speaks to someone, only they hear His voice because it's meant for them only. When God wants a person to hear the word of God, he uses another person's voice—but, be very careful, because that voice could also be the voice of the devil.

People often ask me how I know when God is speaking to me? I tell them that I have to listen carefully, as I don't know what he's going to say. I also know when God is speaking to me, because He never calls me "Master Jones." Instead, God always refers to me as, "Bill." And, when he calls me Bill, I know I'm in trouble!

People ask me how I know when God is not speaking to them? The answer is, I don't hear anything.

Then, God asked, "Bill do you know how many times I listen to you?" I answered, "Every single time." He then asked, "Do you know how many times you listen to me?" I said, "Probably never—just joking."

Then God said, "Bill, you are the best of the best and the worst of the worst." I was stunned by what He had to say and said, "What?" He said, "Just think of one person on two trains, at the same time, on the same track. That person will meet Me on Judgment Day and I will ask them, 'So, what train were you on?' One of those trains goes to hell and one of those trains goes to heaven."

I then asked God, "What is the name of that train that goes to heaven?" God said, "It's called 'the train of hope.' A lot of people get on this train of hope and pray. They ask Me to forgive them. They stay on it for a short time, then they jump off the train and get on the other train and go back to where they began. They start doing the same things that they asked Me to forgive them for in the first place, and never end up following the direction that I have already prepared for all of them on the train of hope."

Then God stopped speaking. I woke up the next morning which was Easter. God began speaking again and said, "So Bill, what train are you going home on this morning?" I said, "Well, I have prayed for three days to find a straighter path to you. I am getting on the train of hope."

God then said to me, "Bill, you can stay on that train for as long as you'd like. It will take you as far as you'd like to go—all the way to Heaven."

God gives us a choice of which path to follow, but there is only one path to God himself.

And he said, Go forth, and stand upon the mount before the LORD.
And, behold, the LORD passed by, and a great and strong wind rent
the mountains, and brake in pieces the rocks before the LORD;
but the LORD was not in the wind: and after the wind
an earthquake; but the LORD was not in the earthquake:
And after the earthquake a fire; but the LORD was not in the fire:
and after the fire a still small voice. And it was so,
when Elijah heard it that he wrapped his face in his mantle,
and went out, and stood in the entering in of the cave.
And, behold, there came a voice unto him, and said,
What doest thou here, Elijah?
1Kings 19:11-13

CHAPTER 12
The Little Black Hand

When I went camping one time, I heard strange noises down by the lake for several days. It sounded like Geese. I was busy praying and enjoying myself so I didn't go down to check. A few days later, I went down and discovered that it was thousands of fish jumping in the water. It was one of the most amazing things I had ever seen.

They were carp fish, and they were doing what is called "rolling." The water was only a foot deep and it was really strange because I could walk clear across the lake. There were thousands of fish, all around me, rolling. I put my hands in the air and started praying to God. I suppose I looked like a holy man because I had my hands up and it looked like I was standing on top of the water.

As I said, the water was only about a foot deep, all the way out in the middle of the lake, and thousands of fish were jumping around me. People were staring at me from the beach. I'm sure they were thinking, "Wow, look at that man. He looks like Jesus, walking across the water with thousands of fish jumping around him. This is one of the most amazing things I've ever seen." I was laughing my head off as I thought it was pretty funny. The water was so shallow that boats could not get out to where I was. Nobody knew the water was only a foot deep.

At the time, I had my fishing pole and my net in my hands, and yet, even with all those thousands of fish around me, I couldn't catch any of them. I thought maybe I would just throw my line out and hook one, but God said, "I don't want you to snag the fish because that wouldn't be right." So I didn't. But then I thought that since I had a net, maybe I could scoop one of them up. But, God said, "Bill, that would not be right, either." So I obeyed, and didn't try to scoop them up either. God then allowed one fish to come to the surface so that I could see what kind of fish it was.

After being out on the middle of the lake for a while, I decided to leave and go back to my camp site. Then, later that night, I went fishing. I said, "God, please let me catch a fish today. If you let me catch a fish, I promise I won't keep it but I will let it go and put it back in the water, I promise."

I began fishing when all of sudden, I caught a huge catfish. Even though I had promised God I wouldn't keep any of them, this fish was so big, I decided to keep him. I put him on a rope and put it back in the water. But as I started slowly lowering the fish into the water, a little tiny hand, about as big as my little finger, slowly reached out from under the pier and grabbed the rope and pulled the fish underneath the pier. I grabbed the rope immediately and started pulling and pulling but I couldn't get the fish from under the pier. Something or someone under the pier must have been huge and wouldn't let go. After a while I was finally able to pull the fish up. I checked to see if it had been eaten, but it was still fine and untouched. I thought, wow what was that? It took me about five minutes to pull the fish up. Whatever had hold of it was very strong.

I then walked down to the other side of the pier. I started to again slowly lower down the fish into the water. Suddenly, once again, that tiny, little hand reached out of the water and grabbed the rope and pulled the fish back under the pier. Again, I tried to pull the rope and fish back up but something was pulling back. It was so, so very strong. I pulled and pulled and pulled. Then, finally, I was able to pull the fish back up from under the pier. I checked again to see if it was eaten. I thought it might be something like a bear under the pier, because it was so strong.

I then came up with a plan to see if I could find out what was after my fish. I put the fish on top of the pier and waited, to see what it could be. Maybe it would come to the top where I could see it.

I kept fishing but kept my eye on the corner of the pier where the catfish was. Suddenly, a tiny, little face appeared. It was a little, baby raccoon! But, there was no way that that one little tiny raccoon could be that strong. I lay down and looked underneath the pier to see if there were more of them, but I didn't see anything.

Then, I remembered my promise. I had promised God that I wouldn't keep any of the fish I caught, so I took the fish off the rope and I let it go. I went back to my campsite and prayed to God, to thank him for letting me catch the fish. I then asked Him for forgiveness for breaking my promise.

The morale of this story is: When you promise anyone, especially to God, you must always keep your promise.

Ask, and it shall be given you;
seek, and ye shall find;
knock, and it shall be opened unto you:
For every one that asketh receiveth;
and he that seeketh findeth;
and to him that knocketh it shall be opened.
Matthew 7:7-8

CHAPTER 13

The Fisherman

After my mom, dad and brother died, my sickness began getting worse, and I started losing hope and faith in God.

One day I went to the mountains and I asked God to please tell me a story. Obviously, God has experienced many things, so what kind of story would God tell me?

God said, "There was an old man, a very old man—about 85 years old. He loved to go fishing and camping with his mother and father but he loved to catch fish more than anything because he used to catch lots and lots of fish. But the man hadn't caught a fish himself since he was a young boy—nearly nearly 80 years. Even so, he still loved to fish more than anything in the world even though he hadn't caught a fish for eighty years. So, he still went camping and fishing.

He prayed to God every day, and still believed that one day he'd catch a fish. One day when he went camping and fishing, he looked up to God and said, "God, please let me catch a fish— just one fish, before I die. I promise I won't surrender and I won't give up." Then, the man put his fishing pole in the water and fished for hours and hours and hours, but he still wasn't able to catch any fish.

Just as he started to give up, his fishing pole took off like crazy. He then said, "Remember God, I promised if you let me catch a fish I wouldn't give up—I wouldn't surrender, I promise." After he struggled with the fish for a couple hours he got the fish close to the bank and he reached down to grab it.

God then paused for a minute and stopped telling me the story. He took a deep breath and then continued, and said, "Yes, then the man slipped and fell in the water." God then paused again, took another deep breath and said, "Yes, then several days after he fell in the water, he floated up to the surface, dead. When the people found him, they turned him over and realized that he still had the fishing pole in his hands. The man had caught something, and when the people reeled-in the line, they discovered he had caught the biggest fish anyone had ever seen."

What God was trying to tell me was that if you believe and have faith in Him and never give up, He will fulfill all your dreams in time. It was not about the fisherman, it was about me. God was trying to remind me not to give up, and not to surrender, because at that time, I was suffering many illnesses and injuries and wanted to give up, and was beginning to lose my faith in God.

Delight thyself also in the LORD;
and he shall give thee the desires of thine heart.
Psalm 37:4

CHAPTER 14
The Butterfly

One day I went to the mountains to be alone with God. I looked up to God and said, "God, I have been here for three days and you haven't taught me anything yet." God said, "Do you know what it means to be free?" I answered God, "No, I don't really know what it means to be free. Please tell me." God said, "What if you have no mother of father, no brother or sister, and no job responsibilities? What if you have no where to go and nothing to do? What if you are fee—free like the wind? When the wind blows to the right, it goes to the right. When it blows to the left, it goes to the left. It goes when it goes, and stops when it stops. It goes where ever it likes to go, because it is free."

I said to God, "I still don't understand. What does it mean to be free? You're not free, as you have all of us to care for. And I am not free, because I have all the responsibilities that you have me do here on earth, so what does it mean to be free?"

About this time, a beautiful butterfly landed nearby, and God said, "It is the butterfly. It is born without a mother or father, brother or sister. It has no job. No responsibilities. It has nowhere to go, and nothing to do. Free like the wind. When the wind blows him to the right, he goes to the right. When the wind blows him to the left, he goes to the left. He goes when he goes and stops when he stops. He goes where ever the wind goes. He is free like the wind. Before the butterfly is transformed into the spirit of God, he is a caterpillar that crawls across the dirt. When he is transferred into the world of God, it turns into a butterfly that flies like the angels in the heavens."

I then read many scriptures from the Bible, but still did not truly understand what God meant when He said what it is to be free.

If the Son therefore shall make you free,
ye shall be free indeed.
John 8:36

CHAPTER 15
Life without God

I went up into the mountains to go camping and to spend some time alone with God. I looked up and said, "Wow, look at all the beautiful things created by God; the clouds, the blue sky, the flowers, trees, green grass, squirrels, butterflies, the fish and deer." It was so incredibly beautiful!

Then God spoke to me saying, "Do you know what it would be like without Me?" I answered, "Well, I suppose most people would say it could be like this, or that it could be like that, but I really don't know what it would be like without You, God."

God said, "Close your eyes and put your hands over your ears. How do you feel now?" I said, "I feel empty. So, that's what it would feel like without God—empty."

Then God asked, "What if you could hear everything and see nothing? How would you feel then?"

"I suppose I would feel half empty," I said.

"And, what if you could hear nothing and see everything? How would you

Feel then?" God asked.

 I said, "I would feel half empty."

That's what it would feel like if you have God only halfway in your life.

What God was trying to explain is that there is no halfway to God. You choose to follow God all the way, or not at all. Your life will either be empty or full of all of God's blessings. The only way is to follow God's Commandments. Remember, there is no halfway to God.

I am the vine, ye are the branches:
He that abideth in me, and I in him,
the same bringeth forth much fruit:
for without me ye can do nothing.
John 15:5

CHAPTER 16
The Lake Swim

I used to love to go to Lake Berryessa and swim across the lake. It is about a half-mile across. It was my personal time to just think about my life and about God.

One time, while I was swimming across the lake, I tried to imagine what it would be like if I was on my journey to Heaven. I thought about how much time it took—to swim across the lake, compared to the time of living a full life. It used to take me about a half hour to get across the lake, but the journey to heaven may take a lifetime.

As I was swimming across the lake, a large boat drove by and created big waves. I heard God's voice saying, "Remember, there will be many obstacles in your way. You may even struggle."

The journey to heaven is very complicated and will have many challenges. Many times, when someone is dying and they begin their journey to heaven they don't really want to go yet. They then notice that if they look back to where they started, the journey is much shorter than going forward, so they turn around and go back.

After I had been swimming for long time, God said, "Remember, don't look back. If you look back and realize after an hour of swimming that you haven't gone very far, you'll realize again that the journey is much shorter and turn back. Remember the journey to Heaven may take a lifetime but it will be worth it."

I closed my eyes because that way you don't really know how long it will take to get to the other side. I swam for what seemed like a very long time. I thought to myself, how much farther do I have to go? This is taking me too long. Maybe I should turn around and go back. I then opened my eyes and realized that I was just a couple feet from the other side.

When I had my eyes closed, I asked myself, "What will heaven look like when I get there? Will it have stars or skies, trees, or water? Could the rocks there be blue? Will there be anybody else there? We really can't imagine what heaven will look like.

As I got to the other side, I got out of the water, sat down, and rested. I thought, "Wow, that journey was very hard." At that time, there were about 50 geese, screaming, hollering, and yelling. I said, "Just listen to all that noise!" God said to me, "Quit complaining! They are celebrating because you finally made it to the other side—heaven."

Remember the journey to heaven may be very difficult and have many challenges. We have to continuously change what we do and say—our beliefs, our faith and many things to find a straighter, clearer path to God. Never give up, and continuously strive. Always look forward. Look for the future to come for it in the future where you will find heaven. Amen.

Brethren, I count not myself to have apprehended:
but this one thing I do, forgetting those things which are behind,
and reaching forth unto those things which are before...
Philippians 3:13

CHAPTER 17
The Four Elements

I woke up one morning at camp. Just out of curiosity, I asked God, "So, what do you want for breakfast?" You never know what God might say. I believe that I hear God's voice every day. God answered, "Do you know what the four elements of Earth are?" I said, "Yes; water, earth, fire and wind."

God said, "What do you think about when you think of these elements?"

I said, "For water, I think of waterfalls and lakes. For the Earth, I think of all the things on it, like trees, flowers, and all of God's creations. For fire, I think of candlelight and campfires. And for the wind, I think of a soft, cool breeze on a summer day."

The God said, "Good. This is how you look at it when it is represented by God's softness. But under God's strength, these elements are immeasurable."

I said, "Please explain what you mean."

God answered, "Water means floods—a tsunami. Earth is slides and earthquakes. Fire is unstoppable and death. Wind is tornadoes and hurricanes.

I could not really understand why God would allow these things to happen because they cause destruction and even death. So I asked God if maybe he could explain it to me differently, so I could better understand.

He said, "Hurricanes are to clean the ocean and create oxygen for the fish. Tornadoes purify the world's atmosphere and clean the air. Tsunamis strip the land and make the land fertile again so it can grow crops and food. Earthquakes are to change the environment and make things new. Many of these disasters were created to allow the world to be more fruitful and abundant."

It hurts God's heart to see His people suffer here on earth so He removes all the people who are dying. People who are very old and weak; the sick and hungry, and the   people with diseases—He takes them to heaven where they can live a better life.

But remember, Earth represents the beginning and the end of all things created by God. Like people, or a tree—we begin from nothing, and end up as nothing. Many times things happen in life that we don't understand, but God always has a reason and a purpose for everything. Trust in God, for things are possible.

I call heaven and earth to record this day against you,
that I have set before you life and death, blessing and cursing:
therefore choose life, that both thou and thy seed may live:
That thou mayest love the LORD thy God,
and that thou mayest obey his voice,
and that thou mayest cleave unto him:
for he is thy life, and the length of thy days:
that thou mayest dwell in the land which the LORD sware
unto thy fathers, to Abraham, to Isaac, and to Jacob, to give them.
De 30:19-20

CHAPTER 18

God said it will serve Me
more than it will Serve You

It was Labor Day weekend, which was my birthday. I decided to go camping and fishing with my family. Normally, I would catch many big fish right away, but this year I did not catch any fish at all this year.

That night I went back to the lake to try again. I looked up to God and said, "Please God, let me catch a big fish for my birthday." I then caught a twelve pound catfish. I said to God again, "Now that you're listening God, I want to catch one of the biggest catfish I have ever caught." I then caught a twenty-pounder! I put them on a rope, and lowered them into the water and went back to my campsite.

In the morning, I took my family down to see the big fish I had caught the night before. As I lifted the big fish up, everyone could see them. There were many people renting boats and jet skies and enjoying themselves on the beach. I heard a voice from the crowd that said, "It's a breeder." I didn't think about it and just put the Fish back in the water.

After a while, everybody wanted to see the fish again, so I lifted the rope to show everybody. Then I heard the voice again saying, "It's a breeder. What are you going to do with it?" I answered, "I'm going to eat it." It was a big fish and it could feed my entire family.

Then I looked closely at the fish and noticed that the biggest one was a female, and that there was a possibility that it was going to have babies very soon. So I decided to take both of the fish off the rope and let them go.

I didn't know what God was trying to teach me at that moment, but when I woke up in the morning, my little daughter asked me, "Daddy, do you feel the same way about letting the fish go as you did yesterday?" Before I could say anything, God spoke behind me and said, "It will serve me more then it will serve you."

I didn't know what that meant but told my Family that God said that it would serve Him more than it would serve me, but I still did not know exactly what God was trying to teach me.

I then asked Him. God answered me, saying, "It will serve me a lifetime but it will serve you only a single meal." I still did not understand. I asked God to explain further. God said, "Because you let the fish go to have its babies, those babies will grow up and have hundreds of babies that will last for thousands and thousands of years." It would serve God a lifetime, but it would have served me only that single meal. But remember, at the beginning, all God said was that it would serve Me more than it would serve you.

Cast thy bread upon the waters:
for thou shalt find it after many days.
Ecclesiastes 11:1

CHAPTER 19
How I met my Wife

First, my wife read a story to me about a woman in China that wanted to get married. A pastor told her to write down all the qualities that she wanted her husband to have. He then he said, "I will pray for you, but remember every morning when you get up, read all of these things out loud and pray to God for the answer."

The priest left on vacation and while he was gone, she met a man and he was fascinated by her and decided to get married. When the priest returned, he heard the good news about the woman getting married.

That story inspired my wife to write a list of qualities that she was looking for in the man that God would bring to her. This testimony is written by my wife Marie Jones:

> I want to share with all of you my testimony on this special day. I prayed for my husband for years but I learned that God likes it when we are specific in our prayers. Therefore, I began to pray for the qualities that I wanted my husband to have.
>
> I wanted a husband who is a man that: Loves God, likes children, goes to church, is easy going and gets along with everybody, is funny, blonde, has blue eyes, is thin, has a big heart, likes the outdoors, is patient, loving, likes music, likes to be the center of attention, socializes well with others, and is very close to my family.
>
> I was waiting for God's timing, to meet my future husband. I had my sister praying for me, too.

Then I joined a Christian choir, Psalm 100, which was an amazing blessing in my life. Every rehearsal was so powerful. I continued singing and praising God with my brothers and sisters in Christ. My sister confessed to me that she and my niece, Sylvana, had asked God to be the first to meet the man I would marry, so that my sister would have the privilege of introducing me to my future husband.

Then one day, at my friend Jennifer's wedding, I met Bill. He was a Christian, and as we became friends, Jesus was the center of our relationship. Our friendship became stronger. He is a man of God.

Years ago, I asked God to use me as a testimony, so that one day I could share it with all of you. Delight yourself in the Lord and he will give you the desires of your heart. This is a true story! After this testimony was written, Marie began her search.

One day, Marie's brother-in-law was parked outside of my Tae Kwon Do school. His car had a flat tire. I was leaving my school, when I noticed him outside, in the dark. I asked him if I could help. He said, "Sure. Thank you" So, I went back inside and got a flashlight and helped him change he tire. After we were done, he asked me if I had a flyer or some information about my school. I then gave him a flyer.

Months went by and I never saw him again. Then one day, he apparently asked his children, "Do you want to go to learn karate?" They were excited and said, "Yes." He then brought his children o my school and signed them up for lessons.

They trained for about a year. We had testing coming up so the students' parents and grandparents showed up to watch them test. We were also conducting a car wash that day to raise money for the St. Jude's Children's Research Hospital.

The parents and grandparents watched how I worked with their children. I was patient, loving, understanding, and caring for all the students and their siblings and friends who were there. I was later told that Marie's grandmother commented about me by saying, "What a beautiful man! That's the man for Marie."

One day, Marie's sister, Heidi, asked if I would be her sister's date for her friend's wedding. I told her that I would be happy to take Marie to the wedding. Heidi told me that I would have to meet her first, however.

When I arrived to meet Marie for the first time, , she didn't seem to be interested in me, even though it was just a casual, first date to get to know each other a bit. Later, we went to the wedding, which was being held at someone's home.

As we arrived at the wedding, I pulled up in front of the house and let her out because it was cold. I went to park my truck, but when I got out, I was a bit lost because I couldn't remember which house was being used for the wedding, and, Marie never came out to find me.

After a long time, I asked someone if they knew where the wedding was being held. They told me, so I walked to the correct house and went inside to look for Marie. When I found her, I immediately noticed something funny; she kept blinking her eyes. I thought that either she had something wrong with her eye, or… that she was flirting with me! But, it turned out, she only had something in her eye, and I was disappointed.

After the wedding date, I asked her out again, and took her to the park. We walked around the park—at least a couple of miles. She would never hold my arm or my hand; she never gave me a hug, and never really seemed to be interested in me at all. I was wondering if she was normal as she never even really looked at me.

Please understand, I was a very healthy man, and felt that I was, at least, not "unattractive." So, I thought, wait a minute

I'll change my clothes and put on some really short pants so that she can notice my muscular legs! I went in and changed and came back out. I put my foot up on a chair to tie my shoelace, to see if she would take a look at my muscles. I have very strong legs and it would've been hard not to notice.

Praise God, she did take a very noticeable look, and I was greatly relieved to know that she was normal!

So, I asked her for another date. We went to a restaurant and as we were sitting there she wouldn't hold my arm and again, didn't really seem interested. I took her hand and put it on my arm and she would just move it. So then I put her hand on my arm and tried to gently bend her fingers to hold my arm. She just thought I was looking at her nails! "What a strange woman," I thought to myself.

After dinner, we went outside to say goodbye. She said, "I have a gift for you—a book." I said, "I've never read a book in my life." (This now seems funny because now, I'm actually writing a book.) So she took it back. Then, she took her hands and rubbed them together and said, "I'm done with him."

I went home and kneeled down to pray. I said, "I'm done with her." God heard me and said to me, "I could not give you a better woman—a woman of God, a woman of purity. She will not lie or steal from you. She will not deceive you, or cheat on you. She's a woman of God." I said to God, "Okay, okay I'll try again."

When I called her, she didn't call me back for more than a week. Her sister told her, "Every time I go to see Master Jones he always looks so sad. He says that he calls you all the time but you never call back." Marie finally decided to call back. We had another date. No matter where we would go she still would never hold my arm or hold my hand. She would never show affection. I then asked her if she had ever dated a man before. She said, "No." I then realized that she was thirty-eight years old, and had never dated a man in her life.

What an honor it was for me to be the first man she had ever dated. I kept in touch with her for months on end. I knew she sang in the choir and had a beautiful voice. I thought, "What a beautiful woman—what a Godly woman to sing to God. This is the kind of woman that I want to marry."

Months later, after dating her many times, I finally tried to steal a kiss. She never closed her eyes or puckered her lips, and never did give me a kiss. I open my eyes and said, "What are you doing?" She answered, "I'm watching TV." Then I asked, "Have you ever kissed a man before?" She laughed and said, "No, never." I don't think she even realized that I had stolen the kiss. What an honor it was to be the first man to ever steal a kiss from her, so I decided after stealing a kiss, I decided to marry her and make her an honorable woman.

After that, we decided to get married, and we have lived happily ever after. Remember this is a true story—the story of Marie and Bill Jones.

Be careful for nothing;
but in every thing by prayer and supplication
with thanksgiving
let your requests be made known unto God.
Philippians 4:6

Who can find a virtuous woman?
for her price is far above rubies.
Proverbs 31:10

CHAPTER 20
A Star

One day, I went camping at Lake Berryessa. I woke up in the middle of the night and said, "God please show me a sign that I'm supposed to get married to Marie and make her my wife." It was late at night and I decided I had to go to the bathroom. I unzipped the tent and stepped outside. I stretched my arms, and as I looked up to the top of the mountain, I saw a bright light. I thought it was a helicopter or a spotlight, but it was a star—the biggest, most beautiful star I had ever seen. I knew then that this was a sign from God for me to marry Marie. I had seen many other stars, but not one like that. It was huge and truly noticeable.

There are many stories to be told, so I am going to only tell you a few more at this time:

It was wintertime and very cold. I decided to get a room at a motel for my brother and one of his friends, Sean. My brother, Jack, drank a lot. His friend had to go somewhere for a few days, but when he came back, he found Jack laying there on his back with his arms in the air to God—dead. Jack's eyes where still open and his body was blue because he had been dead for an entire day. Sean started crying as he really loved my brother like his own father. He started to pray and look up to God and said, "God, please don't let Jack die like this. Please, God." Suddenly, Jack opened his eyes, and came back to his normal color. He came back to life—thanks be to God!

I had tried everything I could do to help Jack. One time, I let him live with me for almost a year but he kept drinking. When I would go to work, Jack would leave so he wouldn't embarrass himself. He knew how much it hurt me to come home and see him like that, so he would leave and walk a few miles away and sit down to think and pray. Remember, Jack didn't believe in God, so my wife and I taught Jack how to pray to God and find faith.

He realized it was really, really cold, so he looked up to God and said, "God, please let me find my way home to Bill's house." Then a big star appeared and he followed it and made it safely back to my house. When he got there, I was relieved because I was worried and could not find him. He said, "Brother I was lost and asked God to help me find my way home. He showed me a star and I followed it back here."

A few months later, my brother died. I went outside and I looked up to heaven and said, "God please show me a sign that my brother is in heaven." I looked up again and a big, bright star was there.

Before my brother died, I once bought him a fishing pole and fishing license for Christmas, but he died before we had a chance to go fishing. I went camping that year and took his fishing pole along. I cast it in the water next to mine. His fishing pole caught more fish than mine! His caught eight, while mine caught none. That morning I took a picture of myself with all the fish. It was funny because in the picture I was wearing glasses and a hat and I normally don't wear either one of them. The hat said "Jack" on the top of it in big letters. I then realize that I looked just like Jack.

Next, I want to tell you a little story about my mother. My mother was the greatest woman in the world. I would not be the person that I am today if it wasn't for all the beautiful things that I watched my mother say and do.

My mother loved everybody. All the children in the neighborhood would come to our house and call my mom, "mom." She loved all of them, no more, no less, than her own.

One time, I remember my mom was going to work. She owned her own business. As she got there, she looked across the street and saw a homeless person on the train tracks. She asked her friends to assist her, to see if there was anything that she could do to help him. He was very sick and old. My mom asked her friends to put him in her car. She took him to the hospital and paid for all his medical bills. She cleaned him up and gave him some warm clothes, and then gave him a job. His name was Bill.

My mom did so many beautiful things for people, I could write a book just about her. She was a godly woman and a great mom. In my family, I have one brother, three half-brothers, seventeen stepbrothers and four stepsisters. My mom was married four times and my dad was married three times. Even with all the children that my mom had to care for, she adopted three more little girls.

At that time, the man that she was married to passed away. She was trying to raise all the children on her own. As my mom got older, she suffered from many medical conditions. She suffered from Diverticulitis, bone deterioration, and Parkinson's disease. It was hard for my mom to believe that there was a God because she saw a lot of people suffering—especially young people. When I told my mom about what God said about the four elements, she said that that story made it clearer for her so she was then able to understand more about God. She would ask me and my wife how to pray and how to have a relationship with God. She often wondered if God was listening to her.

Eventually, she did find God in her heart and inner spirit. She then asked us to pray over her and pray the words of salvation, so my wife and I prayed for her. At that time she started having more complications and had to go to the hospital. A few days later she died. I went outside that night and I looked up and said, "God, please show me a sign that my mother is in heaven." Once again that big star appeared.

Next, I will tell you a little story about my father.

My father was a great, very successful man. He was a man of

integrity and respect and very generous. My dad would have done anything for anyone, at any time, if they were in need. I wouldn't be where I am today if it wasn't for my father's generosity.

My father was getting older and slowly dying. Unfortunately, e was also an alcoholic. One summer day he had a heatstroke. Sandy had to take him to the hospital. He lapsed into a coma for five days. I went to check on him and prayed for him every day, but he wasn't looking better. The doctors took me and Sandy, his wife, aside nine different times. They said his condition wasn't getting any better, and that we should prepare ourselves for him to die.

I looked at the doctor and said, "Jesus healed without doctors and without medicine. He said keep on praying." I began to prepare my father for God. I cut his fingernails and toenails. I combed his hair, and washed his face. I couldn't get his eyes open to see if there could be a chance, just one chance, if he was still alive. It took me a long time to get him to open his eyes. He shivered and said, "Son, how did you know I was here?" I said, "Dad, I've been here for five days, praying." If I hadn't washed his face and tried to open his eyes, he would've just laid there and died.

After he opened his eyes, he said, "Son, I thought that they captured me in the war and had tied me down and blindfolded me." He thought this because the doctors had both of his arms and legs tied down so he wouldn't fall out of the bed and he couldn't open his eyes.

I was greatly honored that God would give my father a second chance to live. It was very hard for my father to express his feelings towards us—to tell us how proud he was of us, or how much he loved us. As a young boy he and his brother always lived in different foster homes.

One day, as I started to leave, I said, "I love you pops. I'll see you tomorrow." I walked away and had gone quite a distance when I heard my father call out in a loud voice, "I am proud of you son, and I love you." That meant the world to me. During this time, my dad was not alone; he had a nurse with him, 24/7, for many years.

I went to check on him three days later and I found him dead on the floor. My father used to say, "Don't push God off on me." But as he died I opened his mother's Bible and realized that my father wrote a special letter to God. Three days before he died, a priest had come to his house and said the words of salvation. My father did have God in his heart and had found salvation before he died.

That night, I went outside and looked up to heaven and said, "God, please show me a sign that my father is in heaven." Then the star—the big, bright star appeared again.

Later when my brother Randy died, the Star appeared as well. I called his wife and children and I told him that the star represented him looking down from heaven. I told them the story about my other brother, my mom, and my dad. It was very difficult at this time for me because in just eighteen months, I had lost my father, mother, and brother.

Yet, every time I went outside and asked God to show me a sign, that special star always appeared. I then realized that that star was the same one that appeared when Jesus was born. It represents the beginning and the end of all things created by God.

And they said, Believe on the Lord Jesus Christ,
and thou shalt be saved, and thy house.
Acts 16:31

CHAPTER 21
I'm Coming Jesus

When my mother, brother, and father died, it was very difficult for me. At that time, God allowed me to enjoy many things that touched my heart. I don't read and I can't spell, but I'm writing a book. I don't read music, but I sing in the choir at the church. I don't read or spell and don't read music, but I've composed fifteen songs. I only went to ninth-grade and didn't get a high school diploma. I don't have a GED, but I have four Masters' degrees, a 9th degree Grand Master degree and two PhD's in martial arts philosophy, and science. These are a gift from God.

One of the songs that I wrote is called, "Jesus finally told me it was time for me to go." This song was written for my brother Jack because he was very sick and he knew that he was dying, little by little, just like my mom and my dad. And now, even I am dying.

Some of the lyrics in this song are filled with emotion. For you understand what I am trying to say is really something special, because all fifteen of the songs that I have written have a story behind them. To me it's very beautiful and I'd love to share this one with you.

Jesus finally told me it was time for me to go. This is a person that knows that they're fading away, little by little each day. Before they go, God reaches down into their heart and lets them know that they need to prepare themselves before they leave.

Will I get to heaven? God shall only know. This means that none of us really know if we are going to get to heaven—only God truly knows.

So I gave all my love and blessings and had time to say goodbye, but he couldn't stop the teardrops from falling from their eyes. This is a person that is in the hospital and everybody knows that he's going to die. So they all come and visit him and God gave him a chance to give his loving his blessings and even time to say goodbye to all the people he loved.

As they start to walk away, they turn around and look at him to say goodbye and then he dies and everyone starts crying and runs back to him. "I'm coming Jesus. I'm coming Jesus. I'm coming Jesus. I'm coming home today." Jesus stops and wonders: Was there anything that He could do? Could He let him stay for just awhile?

Then God lets him come back to life, and they all stop crying. God gives him another chance to live a little bit longer. This is like when my brother came back to life, and when my father was in a coma and God brought him back. Then Jesus said, "I'm sorry but it's time for us to go; when you get to heaven you will know."

This means God has been waiting for him for a while and gave him an opportunity to stay a little bit longer, but now it's time to leave. Then the man says to himself, "Does this mean I get to go to heaven? But I don't know how to get there."

The song sings..."I'm coming Jesus. I'm coming Jesus. I'm coming Jesus. I'm coming home today." So Jesus sends his angels to help him find his way.

Find time with God to kneel and pray, and pray for all the sunshine and the blessings that come your way. But remember we will meet another day. That means my brother and I will meet again in heaven. And then the song sings, "I'm coming Jesus. I'm coming Jesus. I am coming Jesus. I'm coming home today."

That whosoever believeth in him should not perish,
but have eternal life.
John 3:15

He that believeth on the Son hath everlasting life:
and he that believeth not the Son shall not see life;
but the wrath of God abideth on him.
John 3:36

CHAPTER 22
Trust and Believe

I wrote this song for my children, so when I die somebody, they could play it or sing it. That way, they may feel different when I am gone. They know I've been struggling and falling apart, little by little. I really don't want to live like this, but prefer that God just takes me with him.

The beginning of the song starts like this. *"You must trust and believe that I'm now one of the angels; just look in the heavens and you'll see."* This means that I hope God gives me a chance to be an angel in heaven. And all you need to do is to look up to heaven and know that I am there.

Next, *"You must trust and believe in the Lord our Savior; now he is looking over me."* This means if I was sick or had any kind of illness, when I get to heaven I won't have any of those anymore. When we get to heaven, we are no longer flash but only the Spirit of God himself.

Next it says, *"To look in the heavens and the stars above, you'll know that we're looking over you with all of our love."* This means the stars represent all the people that we love and are no longer with us, and all you have to do is look up and see the big, bright star—the same star that represents my mom, dad and brother—the star that I write about in this book. Then you will know it's me and God, sending all of our love and looking over you.

Next this song sings, *"Don't you worry, don't you cry, not one tear drop from your eyes, because God has a special place for me to be."* That means, I am with him in heaven, and hopefully this will bring you peace in your heart.

The next part of the song says, *"Don't you worry, don't be sad, I'm now in heaven with my mom and dad."* This means that when

I get to heaven I won't be alone. There is somebody waiting for me when I get there. All the people I know and love that died before me are there.

The last part of the song says, *"Don't you worry because the Lord, don't you worry because the Lord, don't you worry because the Lord has a special place for me and you."* That means one day we'll be together again. Amen.

And God shall wipe away all tears from their eyes;
and there shall be no more death, neither sorrow, nor crying,
neither shall there be any more pain:
for the former things are passed away.
Revelation 21:4

CHAPTER 23
Jesus, Please Help Me

When I was going through difficult times in my life, I had an opportunity to compose fifteen songs and one of them is called, "Jesus Please Help Me." It is composed by Diana Fitchett. It goes like this:

"Jesus please help me, please help me, in my time of need. And Jesus, please forgive me, please forgive me, of all my iniquities. Jesus will always be, yes there, there for me. Jesus will always be there for me. Jesus truly loves me, yes he loves me, in every special way. And Jesus will guide me, and will teach me when I kneel down to pray. Jesus…I love Jesus. I love Jesus all of you can see. And Jesus, yes Jesus. Yes Jesus loves you and me. Jesus, yes Jesus, yes Jesus loves you and me, you and me."

This song really helped me know that Jesus will always be there for me during my most difficult times and that he loves me in every special way. But what I learned the most was, the part of the song that says, "Jesus please forgive me of all my iniquities." I didn't know that when family members did things against God in the past, it would affect my life now. So I had to learn how to pray differently.

Now when I ask God to forgive of all my sins, I must also ask God to forgive all of my iniquities. It's really important that we learn how to pray to God—that we be specific in what we say and what we ask for. It is very important to truly understand prayer and how to apply it in our lives.

I particularly like to sing to God. They say when you sing to God and praise him as well, it's like praying twice. Twice the strength and twice the glory! Amen.

If we confess our sins,
he is faithful and just to forgive us our sins,
and to cleanse us from all unrighteousness.
1 John 1:9

CHAPTER 24
Relationship with God

Remember, the most important thing at the end of any lesson is to ask yourself, "What did I learn today?" If you don't remember what you have been taught, you are wasting your time as well as your teacher's time.

The second question you ask yourself is, "What is my strength and what is my weakness?" Then work on your weakness and allow your weakness to become your strength. Remember, it's not how much I teach you, but how much you learn. And, it's not how much you learn but how much you truly understand.

We don't teach you, we only bring you to the point of understanding. Then when you have understood, you have been taught. Remember, teaching and learning are two different lessons. To learn, you must seek the knowledge. To teach you must know the knowledge. How can one teach if he does not know himself? Without a question, how can one grow with knowledge?

Many times when God speaks to me, I really don't know what he's trying to teach me. When I don't understand, I just ask God to explain. While I was writing this book I studied the Bible seven times .God said, "You really don't need to read the Bible again. You just need to listen to what it tells you and apply it to your life." God was trying to tell me that we don't always need to continuously read the Bible. We cannot live with bread alone, we must live daily on the Word of God.

Have you ever just woke up in the morning and said, "So God, what do you want to do today?" If God replies, "Well, I'd like to go fishing," then I grab my fishing pole, because if I'm going fishing with God we're going to catch lots and lots of fish!

Another time I might ask God, "So, what do you eat in heaven? Chicken?" I tell Him I'm just joking. God laughs and says, "You don't eat or drink anything in heaven because when you get to heaven you are not of flesh but only of the Spirit of God himself."

What does it mean to have a relationship with God? God doesn't want you to just pray to him—to thank him for things, or ask for things. God wants a relationship. That means to sit down and have personal time with him; to talk about anything and everything.

One time I changed many different things in my life. After making all these changes, I felt the same – confused and lost. I didn't know what to think, what to do, or where to go. Should I move? Should I get married? Should I close my business? So I asked God to show me my journey or direction in life. God said it was like a mountain with snow on it. That He can't really show me my Journey or direction in life. That It would depend on the choices I made. I had to create my own purpose and direction in life.

All scripture is given by inspiration of God,
and is profitable for doctrine, for reproof, for correction,
for instruction in righteousness:
That the man of God may be perfect,
thoroughly furnished unto all good works.
2 Timothy 3:16-17

CHAPTER 25
Martial Arts Creed

O ne day I woke up and I said, "God, I have read many creeds in this world. Please let me write a creed about all the things I believe in; about all the things I teach and encourage others to do." Ten minutes later, God let me write a martial art Creed.

When I finished, God said. "What took you so long?"

At that time, I had been practicing martial arts for fifty years. This is my creed:

> *The way of the warrior: I will develop and discipline myself mentally, physically, spiritually and emotionally for the better of others and my personal self. I will not smoke, drink, do drugs or do anything that will destroy or affect my mental growth and physical health. I will always maintain respect for myself, my parents, people of authority, and all others. I will only use my martial arts skills in a defensive manner. I will continuously set goals for myself so I have a purpose and a positive direction in life. I will never show a quitting or giving up attitude in my life or my martial arts training, so I can be the greatest Black belt I can possibly be. The way of the warrior: My philosophy of Life, by Grand Master Bill Jones.*

This is the breakdown of what I call "The Martial Arts Creed." There are many creeds in this world, like Kempo Creeds, Karate creeds or other creeds, which specifically point to a certain form of martial arts. But the Creed written by Grand Master Jones was designed to represent another form of martial arts in the world.

Discipline:

Discipline is not something that happens to you, it is something that has to be developed, in you. This means to discipline one's self mentally, physically, spiritually, and emotionally in everything one says and does. If you drink or do drugs you will never be successful in your business, life, education, job, family, marriage or in anything you hope to accomplish. You will not be healthy. You will not live a long life. You will have mental and physical complications, and you will not live a successful or healthy life.

Respect:

Respecting yourself means to make the right choices. If I notice that I am around people who smoke, drink, steal, lie or are disrespectful, I will have to say to myself that I have more respect for myself and decide not to socialize or be around that type of surrounding. It is more important to never show disrespect or dishonor to your parents, even as they become older and become more difficult. It is very important to always show respect to people of authority, such as police officers. As teachers, we often say that we must also show respect to all others. This means, sometimes, we must respect even people that do not deserve respect. We should show respect to them because we are examples of ourselves.

Force:

Martial arts teaches us to use only the force necessary to defend ourselves. It is not necessary to cause bodily harm. The best defense in the world is to avoid the situation.

Setting goals:

It is important to set many goals in our lives, regardless of how small or big the goal. Goals can be measured. Minor goals can be accomplished right away and bigger goals may take a lifetime to achieve. Remember without a goal, we have no purpose or positive direction in life.

Perseverance:

By showing a quitting or giving up attitude, it only gives you an excuse for failure. There are thousands of excuses for failure, but none acceptable. By teaching you to strive though the complications of life, it will teach you to succeed in life itself.

The way of the warrior, as Grand Master Jones has said, is, "I will be the greatest that I can possibly be as long as God shall allow because I know there is still much, much more to learn." Amen.

CHAPTER 26
Eternal Life

My uncle Andy used to say that life is eternal. I think life is like the flow of water. It's not perfect. It flows to the right and to the left. There are the good things and complicated things in life. Life is not a perfect, straight line. Life is like the Yin and Yang—two opposite forces combined together.

God didn't want our lives to be perfect because we wouldn't appreciate it and we would only assume it to be perfect. God sometimes places challenges in our lives so we can become stronger and have a better relationship with Him increases our faith.

Sometimes when the water flows, it hits rocks and begins to turn. It may turn in the wrong direction in life, like toward drugs and alcohol. It might never find the path that God has prepared for all of us. When the water hits the rock, it must go through it, over it, or around it. It never allows anything to stand in its way. It doesn't realize that it is flowing in the direction that God has prepared for it. Sometimes, the flow of water seems to struggle, as if it were flowing up hill, like when life is complicated. Then, when the water goes down the mountains, life is good.

Our lives must be like the water. We must have a goal. We have a purpose and a positive direction in life. The goal of the water is to struggle through all the complications so it can succeed in life and be set free, like the Spirit of Life. The water represents our lives. Death is like when the water reaches the ocean—it is the end of one journey and the beginning of another. Then, there is no more struggle—no more complications—there is only peace and tranquility.

Then God goes by with the clouds and picks up all the water. He takes it over the top of the mountain and sets it free. At that moment, the journey starts all over again, like when we have children. That's why life is like the flow of water. It is a never-ending journey.

Remember to never give up; be like the water. Giving up only gives you the excuse for failure. There are a thousand of excuses, but none are acceptable. In time, even water will make a hole in the hardest rock.

For all flesh is as grass, and all the glory of man
as the flower of grass. The grass withereth, and the flower
thereof falleth away: But the word of the Lord endureth for ever.
And this is the word which by the gospel is preached unto you.
1 Peter 1:24-25

CHAPTER 27
The Tree of Life

L ife is like fruit on a tree. There is good fruit and bad fruit. If you don't pick all the bad fruit, it will spoil all the rest. The bad fruit is all the temptations and all the evil things in our life, like being dishonest, hating others, lying, deceiving, smoking, stealing, alcohol/drugs, and any other negative things that affect our lives.

I look at the bad fruit of life like cow manure. If you don't walk next to it and step in it, you won't get any on you, plus you won't smell like cow manure. Just remember the rotten fruit always falls right beneath the tree. We can't hide all the negative things around our lives and our children's lives. We can only do our best to guide and teach them to understand and know the difference between good choices and bad choices.

Remember, when your children get older, they will do whatever they wish to do. Your children may not listen to everything that you tell them, but they will imitate all the things you say and do. So the only way that your children will make the right choices, is by the example we set for them.

Many times, people complain about the tree of life not being fruitful or having enough fruit. It is more important to appreciate the tree being half-full, rather than complain about it being half empty. For example, one day I went to a restaurant and I asked the waitress for a large glass of milk. She came back and gave me only half a glass. I called the waitress back and said, "Excuse me ma'am this is only a half glass of milk." She said, "Well, when I poured the milk, I realized we didn't have very much left—only a half glass. So, I asked myself, 'Do I tell the man that I have no milk, or should I bring him just the half a glass?'"

So remember, appreciate the glass for being half-full instead of complaining about it being half empty. Appreciate what you have in life, not what you want.

Not that I speak in respect of want:
for I have learned, in whatsoever state I am,
therewith to be content.
Philippians 4:11

CHAPTER 28

Life is Like a Tree

One day I went to Lake Berryessa and decided to swim across the lake to the other side. When I got there, I looked up and saw a very old tree. It was big, strong, and mighty. But then I noticed that the water washed away most of the dirt from underneath it. The big roots of the tree were sticking out but the tree still looked healthy. It was green and still had life.

God said, "Life is like a tree. It begins from nothing and ends as nothing."

As the tree begins its journey, like when we are born, the tree struggles to push itself up through the dirt to come to the top and begin to grow. As we begin to grow, we are very small and very delicate. As we get older, like a tree, our roots stand firm. We then become stronger and self-sufficient.

Then God said, "This tree will not be there next year." I said, "But the tree is very strong. Only some of the branches have broken off." God said, "Those branches represent a relationship with God. Sometimes we break away from God and create a separation." I thought to myself, "How could a tree die so fast if it's still big, green, and strong?" God said, "It is not the strength of the tree that kills it, but the elements of life itself."

For the tree, the four elements are water, fire, earth, and wind, but for me, the elements are how I live my life. At that time, I was struggling between my illnesses and what the doctors told me. I really didn't know if I was going to be here next year either. As I sat there, on the other side of the lake, I could see a lot of people. God asked me, "What if you already died and you were in heaven looking down on earth and seeing your children, your wife, your friends and loved ones. What should you have done before you came here?" I answered, "I would have prepared a well put-together portfolio, and a video to tell my children, wife, and the people I love, how much I love them and how much they mean to me. I would give them words of encouragement and tell them how proud I am of them, and of what they've become. I would take care of my wife. I'd pay for my burial and put away money for my children's college. I guess I would have a lot of things to do."

Before I could say goodbye, God said, "What if I don't take you now? What if I could send you back so you can accomplish all the things you need to do and to prepare yourself before it is time for you to be with me. Remember Bill, I have a special place for you; a place, here with me."

Thanks be to God. This story was written December 14, 2013.

For I am in a strait betwixt two,
having a desire to depart, and to be with Christ; which is far better:
Nevertheless to abide in the flesh is more needful for you.
Philippians 1:23-24

CHAPTER 29
The Bird from Heaven

I called him "The Little Angel." One year during Christmas, we had a very hard time financially. We didn't even have enough money to get a Christmas tree. I went to my business to try to see if there is anything that I could do. I couldn't figure out anything at that time and started to leave.

I was standing outside my business and my wife was inside the truck. I looked up into heaven, lifted my arms and said, "God, what can I do?" About this time, I saw something coming from above in the sky. It was sparkling, like an angel or something, but I didn't know what it was. Then, the most beautiful, soft, white and blue bird landed right in front of my feet. It was a special kind of bird.

I said to my wife, "Did you see that bird right here in front of me?" I didn't know what to do so I reached down, picked him up in my hands and held him in my arms. He didn't try to fly away, which was amazing. I nicknamed him "Angel" because he came from Heaven. I didn't know what else to do, so I took him home.

The next day, I called the Lindsey Museum to see if they would take him but it was during the holidays, just before Christmas, and nobody was there. I called a veterinarian at the animal hospital, to make sure that he wasn't sick or anything like that. The doctor said they couldn't make an appointment until after the holidays—after the New Year, so I went to the store and I bought him a cage, and a little bell to play with. I also got him other stuff that I thought he needed.

The bird always wanted to sit on my shoulder, sing and play. He really loved being with me. He was a very happy, little Bird.

He brought so much joy and happiness to me and my wife during the holidays. We realized that all we really needed for Christmas was each other, our love and to appreciate what we had not what we wanted.

That night, before we went to bed, I put him in his cage. He tried to open the little doors to get out. He started screaming, jumping, and making all kinds of noise, because he knew he couldn't be with us at that time. I put a cover over the top of the cage to help calm him down so he could rest and sleep through the night.

When I woke up in the morning, I realized something was wrong. I didn't know what it was, but I decided that I was going to take him to doctor, no matter what. I set him down on a blanket, on the ground, and went to wash my hands so I could take him. But at that time my wife said, "Look Bill, he's trying to crawl to you." I ran over and picked him up in my hands. I looked at him and I knew there was something wrong. I look up to God and said, "Please God, don't let this little bird suffer." Then the little bird lifted up his head and looked at me. I rubbed his head and he closed his eyes and died in my hands.

This crushed my heart. This was New Year's Day, and we were going to go to a New Year's party with all my students. When I arrived, I started to tell the story about the little bird. It made me cry harder than I had cried in many years. It broke my heart, because as a young child when my dog died, it hurt me so much that I decided not to become attached to another animal ever again, just so I wouldn't experience that feeling again. But I didn't for fifty years.

Sometime later, on my birthday, my daughters decided to buy me another bird but I didn't want another pet. But because it was from my daughters, I decided to take him so I didn't hurt their feelings. The little bird would sit on my shoulders and sing a very special song that touched my heart. He wanted to be with me and give me lots and lots of love. So again I allowed myself to become attached to him.

One day my wife and I decided to go to the movies. When we came back home to check on the bird, we found him dead. Once again, it crushed my heart so much, I didn't know what to say or do. I just cried. I didn't know why God would allow these things to happen to me—to love something and touch my heart, only to have it die.

I asked myself what it was that God was trying to teach me. After a while, I realized that God was preparing me—preparing me for the death of my father. He died one month later. Then my mother died six months after that. Then my brother died, one year after my mother. They all died within eighteen months. Now I truly understood what it means to be free.

I went to the mountain to pray. I knelt down and started crying very hard. All of a sudden it felt like rain drops falling down and touching me, but it couldn't have been as it was summertime. The sun was out and the skies were clear. Then I realized it was God. God said, "It hurt me to look down from heaven and watch you cry like that." He told me I was his child and that it broke his heart. Then his teardrops fell from the heavens and touched my heart and comforted me.

Remember God will always be there during hard times to comfort you.

CHAPTER 30
The Brother's Keeper

When my brother Jack was young, he was a skilled carpenter. He did excellent work. He could build a house from the bottom to the top with no complications—a master in what he did. As he got older, he fell in love with a woman. He got married and hopefully lived, happily ever after.

Sadly though, he was an alcoholic, just like our father, grandfather, brothers, cousins, and even great-grandfather. In fact, many of the Joneses family for the past 200 years died from alcohol abuse. Although I no longer do, I used to drink a little too, but I knew that the devil had consumed my whole family, so I prayed desperately to God to please help me. I didn't want to be one of those people that suffered with alcohol.

I prayed more for more than two years and I didn't give up. I knew that God would set me free. Jack was an alcoholic and he lost everything. He lost his truck, his wife, his home, his job, and became homeless. I would check on him every day to see if there was something he needed. If he was hungry or cold, or if he needed to go the doctors; whatever he needed, I was always there for him and made sure he was okay. He never wanted to go home with me.

He decided to live the life that he chose, even though it was a very hard and difficult life for him. Many times when I found him, he didn't look very good. He sometimes had no water or food for a couple days and became very close to dying. It was very difficult for me to see him this way. I would cry and pray over him before I would wake him up, because I didn't wanted him to see how much it really hurt me.

Many times I would find Jack close to death. Before I could take him into the detox center, I would have to take him to the hospital, then to the detox center. I would then take him to the rehab center, and finally to the shelter.

After a short time he would start drinking again and they would kick him out. He would be homeless again. We would start the journey all over again. I did this dozens of times. But I loved my brother and would do anything for him. My brother used to say, "I don't know what I would do without you." His other favorite thing to say was, "I love my brother more than anything in the world."

Jack was homeless and lived this kind of life for almost 22 years. The last time I checked on him, I found him dead. There were so many things to be said about my brother and about his life, but it would take too long to write after he died. The Contra Costa Times Newspaper wrote a very special story entitled, "My Brother's Keeper to the End," about me and Jack.

The LORD is longsuffering, and of great mercy,
forgiving iniquity and transgression,
and by no means clearing the guilty,
visiting the iniquity of the fathers upon the children
unto the third and fourth generation.
Numbers 14:18

Christ hath redeemed us from the curse of the law,
being made a curse for us: for it is written,
Cursed is every one that hangeth on a tree:
That the blessing of Abraham might come
on the Gentiles through Jesus Christ;
that we might receive
the promise of the Spirit through faith.
Galatians 3:13-14

CHAPTER 31
Jack

My brother, Jack, was a homeless person for about 22 years. He struggled in many different things. Even at the very end of his journey, he had to be put in the hospital's ICU at least nine different times. The doctors used to say they didn't know how he was still alive.

Jack couldn't believe that there could be a God who loved him and wanted him to live such a difficult life. My wife and I, my children and sister-in-law, along with other people who loved him would pray for him. We tried to take him to church to read scriptures from the Bible, but he would not believe that there could actually be a God that loves him.

I used to look for him every day; sometimes in the morning and at night, just to check to see if he needed something. If he was cold, needed food, or needed to go to the doctors, I would help. Whatever he needed me to do, I would assist him. I tried everything that I could to be there for him. He wanted to live the life he chose. I used to find him every day, in over a hundred different places. I would just pray to God and God would lead me to him.

But one time I could not find him. I went to all the churches, hospitals, and detox centers, and yet, for three whole months, I could not find him. I knew that there was a possibility that if I did find him, I would find him dead.

I talked to a lot of the homeless people to see if they had seen him, but nobody had. Somebody suggested that I could walk behind the highway, and look underneath the bridge which was about two miles away. It was the middle of winter and the grass was frozen. It was raining a lot and terribly cold. I was very concerned about him.

Then I did find him, underneath that bridge. He was soaking wet and had passed out. I found his sleeping bag and his blanket but they were soaked. I didn't know what to do, so I took the sleeping bag and his blanket and I went to wash them. I had to wash them three times before they were clean. When I was waiting for them to finish washing, I went and bought some pants, underwear, a jacket, shirt, gloves, and hat. All that I could think of was to make sure that he was warm and dry.

I walked back those two miles and found him still under the bridge, still passed out. I looked over to see a homeless person crying and I asked him why he was crying. He said, "I wish that somebody could love me that much." I asked him if he could please help me take off all of Jack's clothes so that I could put all the warm clothes on him. We stripped him down naked and put on all the dry clothes but I noticed that I forgot to bring some socks, so I took off my own shoes and socks and put them on his feet.

I then walked back the two miles. When I finished closing my business late that night, I walked back those two miles with the clean sleeping bag and blanket. I prayed over Jack, cried, and then covered him up with the blanket and sleep bag to make sure that he was warm through the night.

In the morning, since I knew where he was, I went back to check on him. I wanted to see if there was anything that I could do. He started to cry. He said, "Brother, there must be a God that loves me." I asked him, "What makes you think that?" He said, "In the afternoon he came by and he changed all my clothes. In the middle of the night he came back and covered me with the blanket."

Jack then prayed, "God please forgive me. I do not wish to live a life like this." We prayed the prayer of salvation and he found God in his heart and his spirit.

The last time I checked on jack, I found him dead. I went to the mountains to pray for my brother. I was praying and crying. God said, "Remember, he is like the butterfly. No more struggle. No more pain. No more emptiness. He's now free, like the wind."

But if any provide not for his own,
and especially for those of his own house,
he hath denied the faith, and is worse than an infidel.
1 Timothy 5:8

Bear ye one another's burdens,
and so fulfill the law of Christ.
Galatians 6:2

That if thou shalt confess with thy mouth
the Lord Jesus, and shalt believe in thine heart
that God hath raised him from the dead,
thou shalt be saved.
Romans 10:9

CHAPTER 32
Hard Times

Well before I wrote this book, in December 2013, I really went through a lot of hard times. There were actually too many to remember, but I'm going to share a few with you:

First my dad died. Then a few months later my mom died. A few months after that, my brother died. This was very, very difficult on me. Neither my father or mother left a will, so we had to go through probate, which was tremendously difficult and stressful. It affected me mentally, physically, emotionally, but especially financially.

After I found out what I could do to take care of all these responsibilities I became about $72,000 in debt. Then, I started having physical complications—a lot of them as you have read in other parts of this book. I had to go to about twenty different specialists, who never did help me. One doctor even said that my body was failing. He mentioned that my organs were shutting down, and that I could go blind, lapse into a coma, and eventually die.

That certainly didn't make me feel any better, and I didn't have any insurance at that time, which also affected my finances. About this time, my landlord brought to my attention that my lease was running out and that I had to make a choice to stay there five more years. I had been at the same location for 28 years and my business really hadn't been doing very well for the last few years.

I was emotionally disturbed by all of this and didn't know what to do. Should I sign up for another five year or move? I didn't have money to move so after a while I decided I would stay for the students so they could complete their black belt. I waited for the landlord to send me a new contract and even called him many times, but he never replied.

One day I got a phone call. The landlord said he was giving me two weeks to move and to give him the keys. God told me to move before, but I didn't do it, so He decided to give me a little help. He just kicked me out and threw me to the streets. I said to myself, "My God, how can they do this to me? I've been here for 28 years." Without knowing what to do and where to go, I was totally lost. I looked everywhere and could not find a place for my karate school. I tried to look for a place close by to make it easy for my students so I wouldn't lose all my business but I never found a place. I had very little time left to find out where I was going to go next.

My wife told me of this location at the Dana Plaza. I went to look at the building but the building looked sloppy and dirty. I really didn't want to be there. I started walking along looking at all the other empty buildings in the shopping center. I stopped and looked inside the buildings and as I was going to walkway. One of the mothers from my other school came running out of a beauty salon. She had all this stuff in her hair. She looked scary and she just kept talking and talking and talking. So I kept looking and looking and looking in the empty building. I noticed there were mirrors. After a while I noticed there was little poles where you stretch on like at a dance studio. Then I noticed something that looked cool like a Chinese temple. I realized it was an old karate school.

Then I said, "It's almost the same size of my old school, except it doesn't have any changing rooms." The woman said, "It doesn't need one."

I then decided this is where I needed to be, but I still didn't know how I was going to move because I didn't have any money.

That day the old landlord called me up and said, "I just realized that I over charged you $6000 last year and I have to return it to you. I will be writing you a check. I also realized that 28 years ago you paid first and last month's rent of $2800. I have to give that back to you as well."

I thought, "Wow, now I will have some money." Then the new landlord heard about my old landlord and said, "That is terrible that they would do something like that to you after 28 years. You know what? I'm going to give you two months free." That saved me $6000. He let me move in right then.

I began moving. Everybody helped me—all of my students' parents and every friend. It was a beautiful thing to see all the people supporting me.

Then I had to go to another specialist for my health. He wanted me to give him some money before he could start, so I wrote him a check. I asked him if he could hold it until I could get a credit card to pay for it but his wife didn't know and cashed it. Then I had to go to the bank to find out where I stood because I didn't have any money. I looked at my bank account and realize that I had $2700 extra. I had no clue where it came from.

I then decided to look at my other bank account and I had $1200 extra in that account as well. I then decided to count the money that I've been saving for my wife when she graduated and realized I had $900 extra in there as well. I said, "Oh my God, what a blessing." I realized I had close to $17,000 to open my new school. we opened the first Christian martial Arts School

Everything we did, from the paint to the building, to the walls, to the signs—anything and everything we did—seemed perfect; hundred of things, miracle after miracle after miracle.

After that was over, I thought, "What am I going to do now with my dad, mom, and brother?" I still didn't have a lot of money, and I was still $72,000 in debt.

After my brother died, the newspaper wrote a special article in the Contra Costa Times entitled, "The Brother's Keeper to The End." It was unbelievably beautiful about how I loved and took care of my brother. A lady from the Queen of Heaven Cemetery read the letter. She called my church and asked questions about me. They told her all about the beautiful things that God allows me to do for the homeless, for St. Jude's Children's Research Hospital, and hundreds of other beautiful things. She said, "What a beautiful man. I would like to do something special for him."

She called me up and asked me to come to the Queen of Heaven Cemetery. As I got there she showed me a beautiful crypt called "The Crypt of the Heavenly Angels." She said, "I would like to put your mother, father and brother here." I asked her, "How much is going to cost me?" She said, "Nothing. I'm going to do this for you for free."

I cried, just like I'm doing now. What a blessing from God.

Next, the lawyers called me up and said, "Bill, your father left you some money after the probate. We have a check for you for $35,000. Your brother before he died wrote out a will. He knew you were the only person that took care of him for 22 years and left everything to you. We have another check for you for $35,000."

This helped me to get out of debt and started my life all over again, debt-free. Sometimes things happen in our life that we don't understand, but for God there's always a reason and a purpose. Thank God that he's always been there for me.

I understood what God meant about the butterfly and what it means to be free.

For ye know the grace of our Lord Jesus Christ, that, though he was rich, yet for your sakes he became poor, that ye through his poverty might be rich.
2 Corinthians 8:9

But my God shall supply all your need according to his riches in glory by Christ Jesus.
Philippians 4:19

CHAPTER 33

The Unknown

One day I was praying and I looked up to God and said "Lord, you haven't talked to me or taught me anything in a while," and then, when I was done, I began walking up the mountain in the middle of the night.

I was imagining what it would be like if I was walking toward heaven and there was no moonlight. It was very dark. I came across an old man and I said, "Excuse me, sir. I am lost and am looking for the trail that takes me to Jesus Christ. Can you help me?"

The old man said "Sure, we can find him together." I said "The trail is washed away and I cannot see it." He said, "The trail cannot be seen." I said, "How will I know when I get there?" He said, "How do you know you're not already there?"

I asked God if he could explain to me so l could understand. Then He said, "If you died and you woke up somewhere different, you would not know the difference between where you were and where you are. You would not know the difference if you were dead or alive. You would only be in a different frame of mind and because you have never seen God himself, you may not recognize him and understand that there could be a possibility that you were standing in the presence of God himself, and the reason that you could not see the trail that led you to Jesus is because you're already there in heaven, in the presence of God himself."

By Grand Master Bill Jones, Mother's Day 2015.

Epilogue

At this point, I would like to share a few stories about things that happened since I began writing this book. It's hard to imagine where I was compared to where I am today.

There was a time when my days were mostly very difficult— only about 25% of any give day could be considered "good." Now, I enjoy about 95% of my good days, which is a miracle. Keep in mind that there is no cure for Parkinson's.

Now, let me tell you one story. As you previously read in my book, I went to priests many times for healing and anointing. But this time was very unusual. In 2015 I went to a healing service with Benny Hinn. There were about 20 ministers laying hands on people and praying for them. I looked at my wife and said, "The lady is waiting for me." She said, "What lady?" I said, "The one over there, one of the priests." My wife said, "But she's not looking at you." But I knew that God was telling me that she was waiting for me, so my wife told me to go ahead and go to her, or to someone else. Again I said to my wife, "God told me she's waiting for me."

I went to her and told her my physical problem. The woman could see by looking at me that I had a severe case of Parkinson's Disease. She started praying for me and then suddenly started shaking, like I do with my Parkinson's. She placed her hands on me and started praying. I began to cry. I felt light-headed. I tried to remain standing, but the power of God was too strong and I gently fell to the ground. I wasn't sure if anybody caught me because when I went to ground I fell very slowly and softly.

There were hundreds of people there that day but I was the only person that fell to the ground and started shaking severely.

I could hear voices as many people were standing around me, speaking in tongues. I don't know how long I was there but when I opened my eyes I was the only person there with one other person waiting to lift me up. I asked the priest, "What were all the voices?"' because there was nobody around me but the man to lift me up. He said it was the angels praying over me.

From that time on, strange things started happening to me. I worked very hard the past six years as I developed different therapies, muscle memory, range of motion, and other things to help me with my disease and effort to try to become better. Now, for the last three months, it has been truly amazing because every day, for up to three hours at a time, God has allowed me to be one hundred percent healed.

It began with just five minutes a night. It then progressed to once a day, then to once a week. Now, amazingly it's twice a day. I am now able to do things that I could not do even before there was nothing wrong with me! It is truly a miracle. God has allowed me, everyday for a short time, to be one hundred percent healed.

This restored my faith, that through God all things are possible. Now I'm able to walk, run, pet my dog's ears, water the grass, stir the coffee, ride my bike, dance, swim, and do many other things that I could not do for the past six years.

One of the most amazing things that happened to me on my birthday in September, 2015, was to swim a quarter mile across a lake and back with a lifejacket. I was able to use both my arms and both my legs without any complications at all. This was truly amazing... so I did it again.

Earlier in my book, you may have read the story of when I would swim across the lake with both my arms and both my legs wearing a lifejacket with no complications. But one time, I took off my lifejacket and immediately went underwater and started drowning, so I was afraid to try again. God told me that I'd be able to do it with my lifejacket, not without. But I knew that I had to truly believe and trust that God would be there for me during my difficult times. So I tried again. I took off my life-jacket, and swam across the lake and back with no complications at all for the first time in six years.

I know now that God has a special plan for me and that he is healing me, and wants to use me as a testimony for God's love. He told me I was already healed, I just needed to recover. At first, I didn't understand what that meant, but as I watch the things I do today, I am truly amazed at the love of God; that through God all things are possible.

ABOOKS

ALIVE Book Publishing and ALIVE Publishing Group
are imprints of Advanced Publishing LLC,
3200 A Danville Blvd., Suite 204, Alamo, California 94507

Telephone: 925.837.7303 Fax: 925.837.6951
www.alivebookpublishing.com